MORE STATELY MANSIONS

by Eugene O'Neill

Shortened from the author's partly revised script

by KARL RAGNAR GIEROW and edited by DONALD GALLUP

New Haven and London: Yale University Press

FIRST EDITION

Copyright © 1964 by Carlotta Monterey O'Neill.
Seventh printing, 1979.

Set in Aldine Bembo
and printed in the United States of America by
The Murray Printing Company,
Westford, Massachusetts.

Library of Congress catalog card number: 64–12655
ISBN: 0–300–00808–2 (cloth)
          0–300–00177–0 (paper)

THE EUGENE O'NEILL COLLECTION was founded at the Yale
University Library in 1931 by Carlotta Monterey O'Neill.
It includes books, photographs, manuscripts, and typescripts,
among them *More Stately Mansions*. All royalties from the
sale of editions and translations of this book go to Yale
University for the benefit of the Eugene O'Neill Collection,
for the purchase of books in the field of the drama, and for
the possible establishment of Eugene O'Neill Scholarships
in the Yale School of Drama.

List of Illustrations

Prefatory Note

The cycle of plays which was to have been the culmination of Eugene O'Neill's career as a dramatist occupied the major portion of the last ten years of his writing life. "A Tale of Possessors Self-dispossessed" was to have traced the fortunes of an American family, the Harfords, examining the effect upon its various members of the corrupting power of material things. Concerning the series, O'Neill wrote in his Work Diary on May 21, 1941: "have not told anyone yet of expansion of idea to 11 plays—seems too ridiculous—idea was first 5 plays, then 7, then 8, then 9, now 11!—will never live to do it—but what price anything but a dream these days!" He had then completed first (longhand) drafts of the first four plays and had prepared notes and outlines for the five remaining plays of the nine-play Cycle. But the first two plays were much too long, as he had admitted to himself on October 20, 1940: " . . . both as long as 'S[trange]. I[nterlude].'—too complicated—tried to get too much into them, too many interwoven themes & motives, psychological & spiritual". The decision six months later to expand the two plays into four was his desperate solution to the otherwise insoluble problem of how to reduce them to actable length. Although he subsequently prepared notes for this contemplated expansion and actually rewrote parts of the third and fourth plays in accordance with the new plan, sickness, and despair at the state of the world kept him from realizing his dream: he and Carlotta burned the scripts of "Greed of the Meek" and "And Give Me Death," the first two plays of the nine-play Cycle, at Tao House on February 21, 1943.

But although O'Neill had failed to achieve his hopes for the Cycle, he had succeeded before 1943 in completing to his satisfaction the third play of the series, *A Touch of the Poet* (written 1936, published 1957), and had partly finished his extensive revision of a third draft of the fourth play, *More Stately Mansions*.* And he had interrupted work on the Cycle plays to write *The Iceman Cometh* (written 1939, published 1946), *Long Day's Journey into Night* (written 1940, published 1956), *Hughie* (written 1941, published 1959—the first of a projected series of one-act plays to be entitled "By Way of Obit"), and *A Moon for the Misbegotten* (written 1941-42, published 1952), his last work.

* The title is from Oliver Wendell Holmes' "The Chambered Nautilus." It will be noted that O'Neill has Simon quote from it in 1841 (Act Three, Scene One) although the poem was not published until 1858.

vii

Abigail

Abigail (looks around the clearing - bitterly)   And I hoped he
would be here, eagerly awaiting me (She forces a self-mocking smile)
What can you expect, Abigail?   At your age, a woman must become
resigned to wait upon every man's pleasure, even her son's.
(She picks her way daintly through the long grass toward the bench, and I
answering herself resentfully)   Age?   I am only forty-five. and I
do not look more than thirty.   I am still beautiful.   You harp on
age as though I were a withered old hag!   (Mocking again)   Oh, not yet,
Abigail!   But now that the great change in a woman's life is upon you,
it would be wise of you, I think, to look ahead discipline your
mind to accept this fate of inevitable decay with equanimity.   (She
gives a little shiver of repulsion - determinedly)   No!   I will not
think of it until my mirror compels me!   I still have years before me.
(She breaks a leaf off the branch fastidiously and sits down - sneeringly)   And what will you do with these years, Abigail?   Hide from
life and dream them away as you have all the other years since Simon
deserted you?   Live in the fake life of books, in histories of the past?
Continue your present silly obsession with scandalous French Eighteenth
Century memoirs?   Dream yourself back until you live in them an imaginative life more real to you than reality, until you become to yourself
not the respectable, if a trifle mad, Mrs. Henry Harford, wife of the well
known merchant, but a noble adventuress of Louis's Court, and your little
walled garden the garden of Versailles, your pathetic ugly summerhouse
a tiny Temple of Love the King has built as an assignation place where
he can keep passionate tryst with you, his mistress, the unscrupulous

sorry with sneering self-mockery - tauntingly)   Really, Abigail, this
latest day dream is the most absurd of all the many ridiculous fantasies
in which you have hidden from yourself!   I begin to believe that truly
you must be more than a little mad!   ~~And unless you~~   One
day you may ~~become so~~ deeply ~~lost~~ in that romantic ~~dream~~ of evil, you
will not ~~be able to~~ find your way back ~~to yourself~~.   (Answering herself
with defiant bravado)   Well, let that happen!   I would welcome losing
myself forever!   (~~Then with a little shudder of dread~~)   But you are
talking nonsense!   As if there ever could be any danger!   I am mistress
of my own mind, and unless I deliberately willed it -   (With a strange,
morbid conviction)   Oh, I could if I willed it, I grant you!   There
are times when I feel that escape would be as simple as opening an in-
~~sanity~~ door and stepping across the threshold.   (Abruptly - angry)
But you ~~do~~!   ~~You~~ distort and exaggerate, as you always do!   You know
I do not take ~~this daydream~~ seriously.   I am lonely-desperately lonely
and bored!   I am disgusted with watching my ~~ailing~~ revolting body decay,
~~forced~~ to day.   Anything to ~~distract~~ my mind and forget myself.   -to
while away the time -   (Her other self seeks it tauntingly)   Yes, the
little time remaining to you of ~~your~~ beauty.   Abigail, you spend in
childish romantic make-believe, while life ticks round the clock in receding footsteps of farewell -   (Strong - determined)   Not   You know I
have determined to abandon dreams, to live in the future - in the rest in life
in the little time remaining -   Else why am I here now?   Why did I
so lower my pride as to write and beg Simon when his lukewarm cold
nothing of wanting to see me?   (Answering herself)   Why?   Don't ask -!
me, Abigail.   I cannot imagine what you hope to accomplish by
(Interrupting herself hurriedly)   Besides, ~~you know~~ very well there is
a perfectly rational explanation ~~of the daydream you pretend to despise~~.
I have seriously taken up the study of Eighteenth Century France to
occupy my mind.   I have always admired the Bourbons, ~~in spite of their~~

The first notes for *More Stately Mansions* were made in February 1935, and the first (longhand) draft of the play, in four acts and an epilogue, was finished on September 8, 1938. O'Neill recorded the fact in his Work Diary with the comment: " . . . needs lot of revision & rewriting—is as long as Strange Interlude!—but don't think will be able to cut length much". The second (longhand) draft was completed on January 1 and the third (first typed) draft on January 20, 1939. Further revisions and notes for rewriting were made in 1940 and 1941, and O'Neill was sufficiently satisfied with the play for the typescript to escape destruction when both longhand drafts were burned along with the first two Cycle plays in February 1943. He did, however, take the precaution of writing on a leaf laid into the typescript: "Unfinished Work This script to be destroyed in case of my death! Eugene O'Neill".

In 1951, when both Eugene and Carlotta Monterey O'Neill were ill and the house at Marblehead was about to be sold, this revised typescript of *More Stately Mansions* was inadvertently included in a large box of papers sent to the O'Neill collection at Yale. Because the Library understood that unpublished manuscripts were not to be made available to scholars, no question was raised with Mr. and Mrs. O'Neill concerning the typescript. After Mr. O'Neill's death in 1953, Mrs. O'Neill asked that all material relating to the Cycle be restricted for a period of twenty-five years and again there seemed to be no reason to ask about the eventual disposition of *More Stately Mansions*. In May 1956, after *Long Day's Journey into Night* had been published and the arrangements for the publication of *A Touch of the Poet* had been concluded, Mrs. O'Neill telephoned me (in my capacity as curator of the O'Neill collection) to ask whether there were in the collection any other completed scripts beside the one-act play *Hughie,* and I of course reported to her the existence of the typescript of *More Stately Mansions*. She had been under the impression that all drafts of the play had been destroyed in 1943 and asked me to return the typescript to her. I returned it on May 16, having first removed and retained in the collection the instruction leaf that O'Neill had laid into it. In the Spring of 1957, Mrs. O'Neill informed Karl Ragnar Gierow, then Director of the Swedish Royal Dramatic Theatre, of the existence of the play and eventually gave him permission to attempt to shorten the script for possible production in Swedish translation at the theatre in Stockholm where *Long Day's Journey into Night* had been first presented. There was at that time no question of its publication, either in Swedish or in English. Mr. Gierow took the typescript with him to

Sweden, had it photographed there, and returned the original to Mrs. O'Neill, who, on April 8, 1959, gave it back to the Yale Library.

After five years Mr. Gierow succeeded in making an acting version, guided in part by the author's own notes, but following Mrs. O'Neill's stipulation that only O'Neill's words could be used. He omitted entirely the first scene of Act One (combining the remaining scene of that act and the two scenes of Act Two into a single act) and the Epilogue. These had provided links with *A Touch of the Poet* and "The Calms of Capricorn," the plays coming, respectively, just before and after *More Stately Mansions* in the Cycle. Mr. Gierow omitted also the early part of the second scene of Act Three (now Act Two), in which Sara's four sons appear on stage with their grandmother. Otherwise his cuts were confined to words, phrases, and passages here and there, including much of O'Neill's description of characters and sets, many of his stage directions, and most of the references to the contemporary American scene. When this shortened version was produced in Stockholm for the first time on November 9, 1962, Mr. Gierow was able in the printed program to assure the audience that "There is not a scene, not a passage, not a line in the drama which is presented tonight that is not by O'Neill himself."

Mrs. O'Neill now feels that this play should be produced in future only in the repertory of the Swedish Royal Dramatic Theatre, but she has agreed that its text may be made available for students of O'Neill's work. Because Mr. Gierow made his version by shortening the translation of the complete script that he and Sven Barthel had prepared, the equivalent in O'Neill's words of the Swedish version had to be established by comparison with the original English script. For this work I am responsible.

It was at once apparent that in a reading version much more of O'Neill's visualization of the characters and the settings should be included than had been used in the acting script, copies of which had been distributed only to members of the cast and others directly concerned with the production of the play. With Mr. Gierow's approval, I have restored some other short passages not in the Swedish version, chiefly in order to make certain transitions less abrupt for the reader, and have omitted a few lines included in the Swedish version. I have kept my editing of O'Neill's text to an absolute minimum and have changed or added not more than perhaps a dozen words all together. Obvious mistakes, including spelling and typing errors, have been corrected; punctuation has been made uniform to a certain extent; but otherwise the words are as O'Neill wrote them.

The play as now published represents less than half of O'Neill's complete typed script, although the author himself had marked substantial parts of this for deletion. (See, for example, the typed page illustrated.) It is, of necessity, far from the finished work that the dramatist envisioned. Had he lived to see the play published and staged, O'Neill would certainly have revised and rewritten extensively, as he always did, in galley and page proofs, and even in the course of production. But *More Stately Mansions* provides, even in its incompletely revised state, a better indication than does *A Touch of the Poet* of what he had intended in the Cycle. Shortened by a friend in whose judgment he had confidence, the text is one which O'Neill himself might well have authorized for publication.

DONALD GALLUP

Beinecke Rare Book and Manuscript Library, Yale University

MORE

STATELY

MANSIONS

Characters

SIMON HARFORD

SARA HARFORD, *his wife*

DEBORAH HARFORD, *his mother*

JOEL HARFORD, *his brother*

NICHOLAS GADSBY, *the Harford family lawyer*

BENJAMIN TENARD, *a banker*

Scenes

Cabin

10 × 15

Cost less 1½ dollars

log cabin

rough door, window, mortise, old bricks

dug cellar

spaded up

a garden near it no beans, potatoes, corn,
peas & turnips —

8 dollars acre — 11 acres no plot —

no animals to be permanent by —

Act One, Scene One

Scene   A log cabin by a lake in the woods about two miles from a village in Massachusetts. It is just before three in the afternoon of a day in October 1832.

The cabin is ten feet by fifteen, made of logs with a roof of warped, hand-hewn shingles. It is placed in a small clearing, overgrown with rank, matted grass. The front of the cabin, with a door at center, and a small window at left of door, overlooks the lake. Another window is in the wall facing right. At the left-rear is a stone chimney. Close by the left and rear of the cabin is the wood—oak, pine, birch, and maple trees. The foliage is at the full of brilliant Autumn color, purple and red and gold mingled with the deep green of the conifers.

The cabin gives evidence of having been abandoned for years. The mortar between the stones of the chimney has crumbled and fallen out in spots. The moss stuffing between the logs hangs here and there in strips. The windows have boards nailed across them. A weather-beaten bench stands against the front wall, at left of the door. It is home-made, heavily constructed, and is still sturdy.

The clearing is partly in sunlight, partly shadowed by the woods.

As the curtain rises, SARA (Mrs. Simon Harford) appears by the corner of the cabin, right. She is twenty-five, exceedingly pretty in a typically Irish fashion, with a mass of black hair, a fair skin with rosy cheeks, and beautiful deep-blue eyes. There is a curious blending in her appearance of what are commonly considered to be aristocratic and peasant characteristics. She has a fine thoughtful forehead. Her eyes are not only beautiful but intelligent. Her nose is straight and finely modeled. She has small ears set close to her head, a well-shaped head on a slender neck. Her mouth, on the other hand, has a touch of coarse sensuality about its thick, tight lips, and her jaw is a little too long and heavy for the rest of her face, with a quality of masculine obstinacy and determination about it. Her body is concealed by the loose dress of mourning black she wears but, in spite of it, her pregnancy, now six months along, is apparent. One gets the impression of a strong body, full-breasted, full of health and vitality, and retaining its grace despite her condition. Its bad points are thick ankles, large feet, and big hands, broad and strong, with thick, stubby fingers. Her voice is low and musical. She has rid her speech of brogue, except in moments of extreme emotion.

She has evidently hurried, for she is breathless and panting. She looks around the clearing furtively. Her expression is a mixture of defiant resentment and guilt. She hastily unlocks the door of the cabin and changes the key to the inside. Leaving the door ajar, she comes stealthily to the edge of the woods at left-front, and peers up a path which leads from the clearing into the woods. She starts and darts back to the door, enters the cabin and closes the door noiselessly behind her and locks herself in. For a moment there is silence. Then DEBORAH (Mrs. Henry Harford), Simon's mother, steps into the clearing from the path.

Deborah is forty-five but looks much younger. She is small, not over five feet tall, with the slender immature figure of a young girl. Her face is small, astonishingly youthful, with only the first tracing of wrinkles about the eyes and mouth. It is framed by a mass of wavy white hair, which by contrast with the youthfulness of her face gives her the appearance of a girl wearing a becoming wig at a costume ball. Her nose is dainty and delicate above a full-lipped mouth, too large and strong for her face, showing big, even, white teeth when she smiles. Her *forehead is high and a trifle bulging, with sunken temples. Her eyes are so large they look enormous, black, deep-set, beneath pronounced brows that meet above her nose. Her hands are small with thin, strong, tapering fingers, and she has tiny feet. She is dressed with extreme care and good taste, entirely in white.*

DEBORAH
Looks around the clearing—bitterly, forces a self-mocking smile.

What can you expect, Deborah? At your age, a woman must become resigned to wait upon every man's pleasure, even her son's.
She picks her way daintily through the grass toward the bench.

Age? You harp on age as though I were a withered old hag! I still have years before me.
She sits down.

And what will you do with these years, Deborah? Dream them away as you have all the other years since Simon deserted you? Dream yourself back until you become not the respectable, if a trifle mad, wife of the well known merchant, but a noble adventuress of Louis' Court, and your little walled garden the garden of Versailles, your pathetic summer-house a Temple of Love the King has built as an assignation place where he keeps passionate trysts with you, his mistress, greedy for lust and power! Really, Deborah, I begin to believe that truly you must be a little mad! You had better take care! One day you may lose yourself so deeply in that romantic evil, you will not find your way back.
With defiant bravado.

Well, let that happen! I would welcome losing myself!
She stops abruptly—exasperatedly.

But how stupid! These insane interminable dialogues with self! I must find someone outside myself in whom I can confide, and so escape myself—someone strong and healthy and sane, who dares to love and live life greedily instead of reading and dreaming about it!
Derisively.

Ah, you are thinking of the Simon that was, *your* Simon—not the husband of that vulgar Irish biddy, who evidently has found such a comfortable haven in her arms! Yes. Why did I come? Perhaps he is not coming. Perhaps she would not permit him. Am I to sit all afternoon and wait upon his pleasure?

Springing to her feet.

I will go!

Controlling herself—in a forced reasonable tone.

Nonsense! He told the servant to tell me he would come. He would never break his word to me, not even for her.

She sits down again.

It is I who am early. I have only to be patient, keep my mind off bitter thoughts, while away the time—with any dream, no matter how absurd—shut my eyes and forget—not open them until he comes—

She relaxes, her head back, her eyes shut. A pause. Then she dreams aloud.

The Palace at Versailles—I wear a gown of crimson satin and gold, embroidered in pearls—Louis gives me his arm, while all the Court watches enviously—the men, old lovers that my ambition has used and discarded, or others who desire to be my lovers but dare not hope—the women who hate me for my wit and beauty, who envy me my greater knowledge of love and of men's hearts— I walk with the King in the gardens—he whispers tenderly: "My throne it is your heart, Beloved, and my fair kingdom your beauty." He kisses me on the lips—as I lead him into the little Temple of Love he built for me—

There is a sound from up the path at left-front, through the woods. Deborah starts quickly and opens her eyes as SIMON HARFORD *comes into the clearing.*

He is twenty-six but the poise of his bearing makes him appear much more mature. He is tall and loose-jointed with a wiry strength of limb. A long Yankee face, with Indian resemblances, swarthy, with a big straight nose, a wide sensitive mouth, a fine forehead, large ears, thick brown hair, light-brown eyes, set wide apart, their expression sharply observant and shrewd, but in their depths ruminating and contemplative. He speaks quietly, in a deep voice with a slight drawl.

SIMON

Mother!

He strides toward her.

DEBORAH

Rising—in a tone of arrogant pleasure.
You have been pleased to keep me waiting, Monsieur.

SIMON

Disconcerted—then decides she is joking and laughs.
Not I, Madame! I'm on the dot. It's you who are early.
He kisses her.
Mother, it's so good to—

DEBORAH

Her arrogance gone—clinging to him almost hysterically.
Yes! Yes! Dear Simon!
She begins to sob.

SIMON

Mother! Don't! You crying! I don't remember ever seeing you cry.

DEBORAH

Pulling away from him.
No. And it is a poor time to begin. Tears may become a woman while she's young. When she grows old they are merely disgusting.
She dabs her eyes with her handkerchief.

SIMON

You're as young and pretty as ever.

DEBORAH

You are gallant, Sir. My mirror tells me a crueler story. Do you mean to say you don't see all the wrinkles?

SIMON

I can see a few. But for your age—

DEBORAH

Flashes him a resentful glance—then forcing a laugh.
It is true, I am well preserved. But how foolish of us to waste precious moments discussing an old woman's vanity.

She puts her hands on his shoulders.

Here. Turn about is fair play. Let me examine you. Yes, you have changed. And quite as I had expected. You are getting your father's successful-merchant look.

SIMON
Frowns and turns away from her.

I hope not! Sit down, Mother.
She does so. He stands examining the cabin. He tries the door—searches his pocket.

Funny, I could have sworn I had the key. But perhaps it is better. It would only make me melancholy.

DEBORAH
Yes, it is always sad to contemplate the corpse of a dream.

SIMON
Answers before he thinks.

Yes.
Then—defensively.

Unless you have found a finer dream.

DEBORAH
How *is* Sara?

SIMON
Well—and happy.

DEBORAH
You are as much in love as ever?

SIMON
More. I cannot imagine a marriage happier than ours.

DEBORAH
I am glad. You have protested in every letter how happy you were. And the children? Sara expects another before long?

SIMON
Yes.

DEBORAH

All this child-bearing—it must be a strain on Sara. Is she pretty still?

SIMON

More beautiful than ever.

DEBORAH

I was wondering if you would bring her with you today.

SIMON

I thought you wanted to see me alone.

DEBORAH

I did. But perhaps I see now it might have been as well—
Quickly.
I had begun to think perhaps Sara might not permit you to come—

SIMON

You talk as though I were a slave.

DEBORAH

Well, one is, isn't one, when one is in love? Or so I have read in the poets.

SIMON

Oh, to love I am a willing slave. But what made you think Sara—?

DEBORAH

Well, a woman's love is jealously possessive—or so I have read—and she knows how close you and I used to be in the old happy days. You were happy in those days with me, weren't you?

SIMON

Of course I was, Mother—never more happy.

DEBORAH

I am glad you still remember, Dear.
She pats his hand.

SIMON

And I am grateful for all you did for us afterwards.

DEBORAH

It was Sara, wasn't it, who insisted on your paying back what I had meant as a gift?

SIMON

She is very sensitive and proud—
>*Hurriedly.*

But she is as grateful to you as I am. She will never forget your kindness.

DEBORAH

I am grateful for her appreciation. Tell me, Simon, do you ever think now of the book you were so eager to write when you resigned in disgust from your father's business and came out here to live alone—your plan for a new society where there would be no rich nor poor. Have you abandoned the idea entirely?

SIMON

For the present. I think of it often.

DEBORAH

I see.

SIMON

What made you ask about that now, Mother?

DEBORAH

This place reminded me, I suppose. And you really should write it. The times are ripe for such a book. With four years more of Mr. Jackson in power—and even your father admits he is sure of re-election—the precedent will be irrevocably set. We shall be governed by the ignorant greedy mob for all future time. Your poor father! He wishes Massachusetts would secede from the Union. One has but to mention the name of Jackson to give him violent dyspepsia.

SIMON

It's ridiculous snobbery for him to sneer at the common people. In a free society there must be no private property to tempt men's greed into enslaving one another. We must protect man from his stupid possessive instincts until he can be educated to outgrow them spiritually. In my book I will prove this can easily be done if only men—

DEBORAH

Ah, yes, if only men—and women—were not men and women!

SIMON

You're as cynical as Sara. That is her objection, too. But I'm afraid I'm boring you with my perfect society.

DEBORAH

I'm only too happy to discover the dreamer still exists in you.

SIMON

I haven't spoken of such matters in so long— You were always such a sympathetic audience.

DEBORAH

I still am. But are you, I wonder?

SIMON

I still believe with Rousseau, as firmly as ever, that at bottom human nature is good and unselfish. It is what we are pleased to call civilization that has corrupted it. We must return to Nature and simplicity and then we'll find that the People—those whom Father sneers at as greedy Mob—are as genuinely noble and honorable as the false aristocracy of our present society pretends to be!

DEBORAH

However, I would still be nauseated by their thick ankles, and ugly hands and dirty fingernails, were they ever so noble-hearted! Good Heavens, did I come here to discuss the natural rights of man—I who pray the Second Flood may come and rid the world of this stupid race of men and wash the earth clean!
She gets to her feet.
It is getting late, I must go.

SIMON

Go? You've just come! Come. Sit down, Mother.
She sits down again.
You haven't told me a word about yourself yet.

DEBORAH

I am afraid, though you might listen kindly, you could not hear me, Simon.

SIMON

I used to hear, didn't I?

DEBORAH

Once long ago. In another life. Before we had both changed.

SIMON

It hurts that you can believe that of me, Mother.

DEBORAH

Oh, I no longer know what to believe about anything or anyone!

SIMON

Not even about me?

DEBORAH

Not even about myself.

SIMON

What has happened, Mother? Is it anything Father has done?

DEBORAH

What an absurd idea! Your father is much too worried about what President Jackson will do or say next, and what effect it will have on imports and exports, to bother with me, even if I would permit him to.

SIMON

Is it anything Joel has done?

DEBORAH

Worse and worse! If you could see your brother now! He is head of the bookkeeping department, which is about as high as his ability can ever take him.

SIMON

I knew Joel had no ability.

DEBORAH

Joel has become a confirmed ledger-worm. I think he tried once to find me listed on the profit side of the ledger. Not finding me there, he concluded he must merely be imagining that I existed. I invited him to visit me in my garden not long ago—

SIMON

What could you want with him?

DEBORAH

Poor Joel! He looked as astounded as if a nun had asked him to her bedroom. And when he came—with the air, I might say, of a correct gentleman who pays a duty call on a woman of whom he disapproves—he determinedly recited impeccable platitudes, stared the flowers out of countenance for half an hour, and then—fled! You would have laughed to see him.

SIMON

Yes, he must have been out of place.

DEBORAH

He was indeed. So you need not be jealous, Dear. No, I have not changed because of anything Joel has done. Hardly!

SIMON

Then what is it, Mother?

DEBORAH

Nothing has happened, except time and change.

SIMON

You seem so lonely.

DEBORAH

Patting his hand.
You know that. Now I feel less lonely.

SIMON

It's hard to believe about you. You were always so independent of others.

DEBORAH

But a time comes when, suddenly, discontent gnaws at your heart while you cast longing eyes beyond the garden wall at Life which passes by so horribly unaware that you are still alive!

SIMON

How can you say Life has passed you by? You—

DEBORAH

While you are still beautiful and Life still woos you, it is such a fine gesture of disdainful pride to jilt it. But when the change comes and an indifferent Life jilts *you*— Oh, I realize I am hardly as bad as that yet. But I will be, for I constantly sense in the seconds and minutes and hours flowing through me, the malignant hatred of life against those who have disdained it! But the body is least important. It is the soul, staring into the mirror of itself, seeing the skull of Death leer over its shoulder in the glass!

SIMON

Shrinking with repulsion.

Mother! That's too morbid!

DEBORAH

Poor Simon. Mothers should never have such thoughts, should they? Forgive me.

SIMON

Are you still as accomplished an actress as you used to be?

DEBORAH

Why, what a thing to say, Simon!

SIMON

I was remembering how you used to act out each part when you'd read me fairy stories. One moment you'd be the good fairy, or the good queen, or the poor abused little princess— That was wonderful. But the next moment you'd be the evil queen, or the bad fairy, or the wicked witch, and I'd be all goose-flesh with terror!

DEBORAH

You were extremely sensitive and imaginative—as a child.

SIMON

What role do you play nowadays, Mother?

DEBORAH

Stiffens, avoiding his eyes and forcing a laugh.

Nonsense! You forget I have no audience now.

SIMON

Teasingly.

Oh, you were always your own audience, too. So tell me—

DEBORAH

You would be horribly shocked if I should tell you the nature of the part I play in my eighteenth-century past!

SIMON

Your old wicked witches led me always to be prepared for the worst!

DEBORAH

Playfully, but with a growing undercurrent of compulsive, deadly seriousness as she goes on.

This is more wicked than any witch. This is real life, even though it be past.

SIMON

Well, out with the terrible secret, Mother. I promise not to be too horrified. Are you an evil Queen of France?

DEBORAH

Suddenly seems to loose herself—arrogantly.

No. I prefer to be the secret power behind the Throne—a greedy adventuress who has risen from the gutter to nobility by her wit and charm—who uses love but loves only herself, who is entirely ruthless and lets nothing stand in the way of the final goal of power she has set for herself—to become the favorite of the King and make him, through his passion for her, her slave!

She ends on a note of strange, passionate exultance.

SIMON

Startled and repelled.

Mother!

She starts dazedly. He goes on quickly.

No, I am not shocked. It is too damned idiotic!

13

She gives a shrinking, cowering movement as though he had struck her in the face.

No, that's a lie. You really did shock me for a second, Mother. Stunned me, even!

He chuckles.

But now I have a picture in my mind of you sitting in your walled-in garden, dressed all in white, so sedulously protected and aloof from all life's sordidness, so delicate and fastidious and spiritually remote—and yet in your dreams playing make-believe with romantic iniquity out of scandalous French memoirs!

He laughs almost derisively.

DEBORAH

Stung to fury, a flash of bitter hatred in her eyes, drawing herself up with fierce, threatening arrogance.

You dare to laugh at me, Monsieur! Take care—!

Then as he stares at her in petrified amazement, she controls herself and forces an hysterical laugh.

There! You see! I can still be a convincing actress if I wish! Poor Simon, if you could see your horrified face!

SIMON

Relieved, grins sheepishly.

You did fool me. For a moment I thought you were serious—

DEBORAH

My dear boy, I hope you don't think your poor mother has gone quite insane! But let's forget my stupid joke and return to common sense in the little time left us. How is your business progressing these days? Judging from your letters, you must be making a great success of it.

SIMON

Oh, only in a very modest way as yet, Mother.

DEBORAH

You hope to do even better? I am sure you will—with Sara to inspire you.

SIMON

Yes, it is all for her.

DEBORAH

I see.

SIMON

See what? I owe it to her—

DEBORAH

Of course you do. But I didn't mean that. My thought was fanciful—that perhaps thus you continued to hide from yourself.

SIMON

You are right to call that fanciful.

DEBORAH

Why, in one of your letters, you boasted that the town considered you the most talented of its young merchants.

SIMON

I wasn't boasting, Mother. I thought it would make you laugh.

DEBORAH

Oh, I did laugh then. Now I see there is nothing incongruous about it. After all, you are your father's son. You are so like him now, in many ways, it's astonishing.

SIMON

Oh, nonsense, Mother.

DEBORAH

One would think you were ashamed of your success.

SIMON

Why should I be ashamed?

DEBORAH

Why, indeed? Unless you regret your lost poet's dream of a perfect society.

SIMON

I haven't lost it! And it isn't just a dream. I can prove—

DEBORAH

Oh, I know. Your book. But you said you had given that up.

SIMON

I said I had had no time lately—

DEBORAH

Four years is a long "lately." But why should you be ashamed of that?

SIMON

I am not ashamed! Why do you keep insisting? Well, perhaps, now and then, I do feel a little guilty.

DEBORAH

Ah!

SIMON

But I remind myself that what I am doing is merely a means. The end is Sara's happiness. And that justifies any means!

DEBORAH

I've found the means always becomes the end—and the end is always oneself.

SIMON

I propose to retire as soon as we have enough. I'll write my book then.

DEBORAH

You have agreed with Sara how much is enough?

SIMON

Hesitates—then lies.

Yes, of course.

A pause. He frowns and goes on moodily.

I'll admit I do get deathly sick of the daily grind of the counting-house— It is not the career I would have chosen. I would have lived here in freedom with Nature, and earned just enough to support myself, and kept my dreams.

DEBORAH

Ah.

SIMON

But when I come home and see Sara's happiness and hold her in my arms, then discontent seems mean and selfish.

DEBORAH

Of course. The danger is that your discontent will grow and grow with your success until— But good Heavens, I sound like Cassandra! Forgive me! And now I really must go, Simon.

> *She gets up and they come to the path at left-front.*
> *Suddenly she says, strangely.*

No, you go first.

SIMON
> *Bewilderedly.*

But why don't we walk together as far as the road?

DEBORAH

Please obey me! You have forgotten me, I think. Can't I be whimsical, as of old, if it please me?

SIMON
> *Puzzled but smiling.*

Of course you can.

DEBORAH
> *Kissing him.*

Goodbye, Dear. Write me frankly of your discontents. I shall be, as ever, your Mother Confessor.

> *She gives him a little push.*

Now go!

SIMON
> *Hesitates—moved.*

I— Goodbye, Mother.
> *He turns reluctantly.*

DEBORAH
> *Suddenly overcome by contrition.*

Wait!
> *She embraces him again.*

My dear son! Forgive me for trying to poison your happiness. Forget all I have said! Have no regrets! Love is worth everything! Be happy!

> *She kisses him—then pushes him away down the path—*
> *sharply commanding.*

Don't speak! Go!

She turns away. Simon stares at her for a moment,
deeply moved, then turns and disappears down the path.
She turns back to look after him.

Bosh, Deborah! He will forget in her arms. I have dismissed that
Irish biddy's husband from my life forever. I shall never see him
again.

As she says this last the cabin door is silently unlocked
and opened and Sara comes out. She stands outside the
door for a moment hesitantly. Then, her face set and
determined, she advances noiselessly until she stands a
few paces from the oblivious Deborah.

SARA

Speaks quietly in a polite, carefully considered and
articulated English.

I beg your pardon, Mrs. Harford.

Deborah gives a frightened gasp, whirling to face her.

I am happy to meet you again—and to know you at last. I was in
the cabin all the while.

DEBORAH

You dared to listen!

SARA

I came on purpose to listen. Though after all I've heard, I know
now I was a fool to be afraid of you.

DEBORAH

Well, I expected you to be low and unscrupulous, considering
your origin, but I never thought you'd boast of it!

SARA

Stung—her inward anger beginning to show, and with
it her brogue, but still keeping her voice quiet.

I have my honor and it's a true woman's honor that you'd give
your soul to know! To have love and hold it against the world,
no matter how! That's my honor!

Gradually losing her control and lapsing more and more
into brogue.

As for what you're after saying about my origin— Don't put on

18

your fine lady's airs and graces with me! I'm too strong for you!
Life is too strong for you! But it's not too strong for me! I'll take
what I want from it and make it mine!

> *Mockingly.*

You to talk of honor when in your dream what are you but a
greedy, contrivin' whore!

> *Deborah shrinks back. Sara goes on more quietly.*

But it's only in a dream! You've the wish for life but you haven't
the strength except to run and hide in fear of it, sittin' lonely in
your garden, hearin' age creep up on you, and beyond the wall
the steps of Life growin' fainter down the street, like the beat of
your heart, as he strolls away forgettin' you, whistlin' a love tune
to himself, dreamin' of another woman!

DEBORAH
Stammers.

That's a lie!

> *She sways weakly as though she were about to faint—*
> *exhaustedly.*

I—I feel a little faint—I

> *She starts for the bench.*

SARA
With an abrupt change to her quiet polite manner and
brogueless English, takes her arm.

Let me help you, Mrs. Harford. You must rest a while.

DEBORAH
Sinks down on the bench.

Thank you.

SARA

I ask your pardon for losing my temper, Mrs. Harford. But the
things you said—

DEBORAH

I know. Please forgive me.

SARA

I came out of the cabin because there's a lot of things I want to
say to you. And I'm going to say them! But before that I want to
tell you how sorry I was when Simon laughed. I could feel it

coming. I waited, praying he wouldn't. When he did, it was like a knife in me, too.

> *Deborah raises her eyes for a second to stare at her with an instinctive grateful wonder. Sara goes on.*

I want to apologize for him. How can a man know about the truth of the lies in a woman's dreams?

DEBORAH
With a faint smile.

I thought you were a fool. I am afraid I am beginning to like you, Sara.

SARA
Embarrassedly—forcing a joking tone.

Oh, don't try to fool me with blarney. You hate me worse than poison. And I hate you. I'm glad I listened. You wanted to put doubt and disgust for himself in his mind, and make him blame me for a greedy fool who'd made him a slave and killed his fine poet's dream.

> *She laughs scornfully.*

It's little you know Simon, if you *are* his mother. Sure, what man doesn't complain of his work, and pretend he's a slave? But if ever you saw him when he comes home to me, so proud and happy because he's beat someone on a sale, laughing and boasting to me, you wouldn't hope you could use his old dream of a book that'll change the world to dissatisfy him. I know what he really likes—the world as it is.

> *She pauses. Deborah sits in silence, her eyes on the ground.*

But what I wanted to say is, you don't know me. I may have a greed in me. I've had good reason to have. There's nothing like hunger to make you greedy. But the thing you don't know is that there's love in me too, great enough to destroy all the greed in the world. If I thought it meant his happiness, I'd live here in this hut, or in a ditch with him, and steal praties from the farmers to feed him, and beg pennies with my children, on the road, to buy pen and ink and paper for his book, and still I'd laugh with the joy of love! I heard you, when he said he'd retire to write his book when we had enough, sneer to him that we'd never have enough.

All I'm dreaming of is to make him retire, a landed gentleman, the minute we've enough, and to bring my children up as gentlemen. You think in your Yankee pride and ignorance, because my father ruined himself with drink and gambling in Ireland, that the dirty inn he came down to here is all I've known. But I was born on a great estate that was my father's, in a grand mansion like a castle, with sloos of servants, and stables, and beautiful hunters. My father was a gentleman, and an officer, who served with honor in Spain under the great Duke of Wellington.

Abruptly.

I beg your pardon, Mrs. Harford, for boring you with talk of my father. He was a drunken fool, full of lying pretensions— But what I've said is true all the same!

DEBORAH

I am beginning to know you, Sara.

SARA

I don't care what you know. Stay in your dreams and leave me and mine alone. Simon is mine now.

Politely.

I must go. Simon will be wondering where I have gone. I promise you I won't confess that. I'll bid you goodbye now, Mrs. Harford.

DEBORAH

Looks up—coldly.

Goodbye. I promise you, in turn, I never intend to see your husband again, or even write to him.

With arrogant disdain.

Do you presume to think I would touch anything of yours?

SARA

No. You know I wouldn't let you.

She smiles mockingly and goes off right-rear.

DEBORAH

Vulgar, common slut! If I wished—if I had the opportunity— No. It is ended—forgotten—dead. It is cheap and mean and sordid like life. I will not let it touch me.

Gradually her tension relaxes, her eyes become dreamy, and she stares before her unseeingly.

21

The Palace at Versailles—the King and I walk in the moonlit gardens— "My throne it is your heart, Beloved, and my fair kingdom your beauty"—

She starts awake and springs to her feet.

No! I have done with that insane romantic vaporing! I will never dream again! Never! I will face change and ugliness, and Time and Death, and make myself resigned!

A bitter ironical smile comes to her lips.

After all, what else can you do now, Deborah? You would always hear his laughter!

CURTAIN

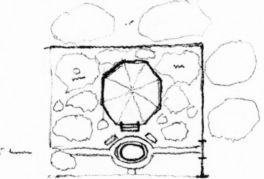

Act One, Scene Two

Scene A corner of the garden of Deborah Harford's home in the city on a warm moonlight night in June 1836.

The corner is formed by a brick enclosing wall, eight feet high, at rear and right. At center is an octagonal summer-house, its walls and pointed roof entirely covered by ivy. At left and right of the summer-house are shrubs, with a line of Italian cypresses behind them along the wall. The shrubs, of various sizes, are all clipped into geometrical shapes—cones, cubes, cylinders, spheres, pyramids, etc. They give the place a curious, artificial atmosphere. In the side of the summer-house facing front is a narrow arched door, painted a Chinese lacquer red. Three steps lead up to the door. Two small stone benches face right-front and left-front, on the edge of a narrow brick-paved walk which surrounds a little oval pool. From this pool two paths lead directly right and left, the left one passing behind a spherical shrub at left-front to the house. The right one leads to an arched door, painted green, in the wall at right, opening on the street. There is a wrought-iron lantern hanging from a bracket in the wall above the door, in which a little lamp burns brightly.

There is a sound of men's voices from down the path off left, and a moment later NICHOLAS GADSBY, *the Harford lawyer, appears accompanied by Deborah's younger son,* JOEL. *Gadsby is a short, tubby man of fifty-six, almost completely bald, with a round red face, and shrewd little grey eyes. Every inch the type of conservative, best-family legal advisor, he is gravely self-important and pretentious in manner and speech, extremely conscious of the respect due his professional dignity. He is dressed with a fastidious propriety in well-tailored mourning black. Joel Harford is twenty-nine, tall and thin, with a slight stoop in his carriage. His face is pale and handsome—the face of a methodical mediocrity, who within his narrow limits is*

*not without determination and a rigid integrity, but lacks
all self-confidence or ambition beyond these limits. His
whole character has something aridly prim and puritanical
about it. He has brown hair, cold light-blue eyes, a
pointed chin, an obstinate mouth. His voice is dry—
prematurely old.*

*They stop as they come to the pool. Gadsby stares around
him, looking for someone. His manner is shocked and
indignant, and at the same time pathetically confused.*

GADSBY

Well? She isn't here. I didn't think she would be.

JOEL
Dryly, indicating the summer-house.
You will find her hiding in there.

GADSBY

God bless me. I cannot believe—?

JOEL

Since Father died she has appeared— well, deliberately deranged—

GADSBY

Come, come, Joel. Naturally, the shock—her grief.

JOEL

Whatever the cause be, it is not grief.

GADSBY

You said "deliberately."

JOEL

You may judge for yourself.

GADSBY

Ridiculous! I have known your mother since before you were
born. Eccentric, yes. Provokingly unconventional. Whimsical and
fanciful. But always a well-bred gentlewoman, a charming
hostess, witty and gay—and beautiful.

JOEL

You are forgetting the business which brings us here.

GADSBY

I wish I could forget. I still cannot believe that your father could—

JOEL

It would be better if you were the one to call her out. I have never been welcome here.

GADSBY

Turns to the summer-house and calls.

Deborah!

He goes to the foot of the steps.

Deborah! This is Nicholas!

He pauses, then turns to Joel uneasily.

God bless me, Joel, you don't think anything can have happened to her?

> *But even as he is speaking the door is slowly opened outwards and* DEBORAH *appears. Her back is to the door as though she had groped backwards in the darkness, her hand behind her feeling for the knob, keeping her face turned toward something from which she retreats. As the door opens, her body, pressed against it, turns as it turns until it faces toward left-front, as the door is two-thirds open. But she keeps her head turned so that she is still looking back over her shoulder into the dark interior. Suddenly a little shudder runs over her; she gives a smothered gasp, wrenches her eyes from the darkness inside, pushes the door back against the house, wide open, and faces front. As he sees her face, Gadsby cannot restrain a startled exclamation.*
>
> *Deborah now seems much older than her forty-nine years. Her olive complexion has turned a displeasing swarthy color. The dry skin is stretched tightly over the bones and has the lifeless sheen of a shed snakeskin. Her black eyes are sunk in deep hollows beneath their heavy brows and have an unhealthy feverish glitter. They appear more enormous than ever in her small oval face. There are deep lines from her nose and the corners of her mouth. Her*

lips appear contracted. There are hollows under her cheekbones and in her slender neck. There is the quality of a death's head about her face, of a skull beginning to emerge from its mask of flesh. Her figure is still graceful in all its movements, and by contrast with her face, youthful. She is dressed all in white.

DEBORAH
Staring at Gadsby—in a low voice that has lost its old musical quality and become flat and brittle.
I am glad you came, Nicholas. I must never go in there again!

GADSBY
There is something in there that frightens you, Deborah?

DEBORAH
Something? Outside me? No, nothing is there but me. My mind. My life, I suppose you might call it, since I have never lived except in mind. A very frightening prison it becomes at last, full of ghosts and corpses. Yes, in the end—and I have reached the end —the longing for a moment's unthinking peace, a second's unquestioning acceptance of oneself, becomes so terrible that I would do anything, give anything, to escape! That is what frightened me. After you called—not before. Before, I was so longingly fascinated, I had forgotten fear. The temptation to escape—open the door— step boldly across the threshold. And, after all, good God, why should I be frightened? What have I to lose except myself as I am here?

GADSBY
God bless me, Deborah, you cannot mean—

DEBORAH
Death? Oh, no. There is a better way—a way by which one still may live—as the woman one has always desired to be. One has only to concentrate one's mind enough, and one's pride to choose of one's own free will, and one can cheat life, and death, of oneself. It would be so easy for me! Like pushing open a door in the mind and then passing through with the freedom of one's lifelong

desire! I tell you, before you called, I saw that door, as real as the door I have just opened, and I was reaching out my hand to—
With a frightened shudder.
I am glad you called. Because I am not sure that one completely forgets then. If I were, I would have gone.
Abruptly.
No, don't fear, Nicholas, that I will outrage your sense of propriety by suicide. I assure you Henry's dying completely disillusioned me with death.

GADSBY

It is very bad for you to come out here to brood over Henry's death.

DEBORAH

Brood? No. But I have tried to make it real to myself. I have said to myself: "Your husband is dead. He was buried this morning. You should surely be experienced in facing facts by this time." Yes, God knows I should. That afternoon at the cabin with Simon seems a lifetime ago, and he is more dead to me than Henry. I have kept the oath I made to myself then. Have made myself accept life as it is. Made myself a decently resigned old woman. Made myself each morning and night confront myself in the mirror and bow a well-mannered bow to Age and Ugliness—greet them as my life-end guests—as elderly suitors for my body, roués in their bored, withered hearts. Not charming company, but a hostess must honor even unwelcome guests. So all day for years I have lived with them. And every night they have lain abed with me. Oh, yes, indeed! I have disciplined my will to be possessed by facts—like a whore in a brothel!

GADSBY

Deborah!

DEBORAH

I have deliberately gone out of my way to solicit even the meanest, most sordid facts, to prove how thoroughly I was resigned to reality. Joel will remember one night at supper when I actually asked my husband: "How is trade these days? I feel a deep interest. Has President Jackson's feud with the Bank of the United States had an adverse effect on your exports and imports?" A silence

29

that shrank back, stamping on its own toes. In his eyes and Joel's a wondering alarm. Has this alien woman gone completely insane? No, she is merely being fantastical again. Deborah has always been fantastical.

JOEL

That is what you are being now, Mother. And we have no time to listen—

GADSBY

He has been staring at Deborah, bewilderedly uncomprehending but disturbed because he senses her despair, and now attempts to regain a brisk, professional air, clearing his throat importantly.

Humph. Yes, Deborah.

DEBORAH

Ignoring this.

And now Henry is dead. I am free. Can't you understand that?

She shakes her head slowly.

No. His death will not live in me. It is meaningless. Perhaps I am too dead myself. The dutiful wife sat by his bedside. He seemed not to suffer but to be impatient and exasperated—as though he had an important appointment with God to discuss terms for the export of his soul, and Life was needlessly delaying him. And then came nothing—an expiring into nothing. Did I think death would be something in itself—a beginning, not just the end of life? Did I expect death to open the door and enter the room, visible to me, the good King of Life come at last to escort one into his palace of peace, a lover keeping a life-long promised tryst? If life had meaning, then we might properly expect its end to have as much significance as—the period at the close of a simple sentence, say. But it has no meaning, and death is no more than a muddy well into which I and a dead cat are cast aside indifferently!

She presses both hands to her temples.

Good God, you wonder I was tempted to open that door and escape! I tell you I am still tempted—that I will not endure being the tortured captive of my mind much longer—whatever the cost of release—

GADSBY

Deborah, compose yourself. This—this is most unsuitable conduct—

DEBORAH

Stares at him—a sudden transformation comes over her. She smiles at him—an amused, derisive smile.

Your rebuke is well taken, Nicholas. May I ask to what I owe the honor of your visit, gentlemen? It is a rare pleasure indeed to see you in my garden, Joel.

JOEL

I assure you, Mother, I would never intrude unless circumstances—

GADSBY

The circumstances are these, Deborah: In going over Henry's private papers, we made the astounding discovery— Upon my soul, I could not credit the evidence of my own eyes! I have known Henry since we were boys together. I would have sworn he would be the last man on earth to indulge in such outrageous folly!

DEBORAH

Outrageous folly? That does not sound like Henry. I think we could discuss this mystery more calmly if we sat down.

She sits on the step of the summer-house, Gadsby and Joel on the stone benches by the pool, at left-front and right-front of her, respectively.

JOEL

We found two letters in Father's strong-box, one addressed to Mr. Gadsby, the other to me.

GADSBY

These letters are confessions that Henry had been secretly gambling in Western lands.

DEBORAH

Gambling? Henry?

GADSBY

Yes, Deborah. Unbelievable!

JOEL

As a result, Mother, the Company stands on the brink of bank-ruptcy.

GADSBY

It appears he had overreached his resources during the past few years—sunk too much capital in new ships—borrowed too freely, and then yielded to the temptation to regain a sound position by making a quick profit in Western lands. He lost, of course. What could an honorable, conservative merchant like Henry know of such wild speculation?

DEBORAH

It would appear I have spent my life with a stranger. If I had guessed he had folly hidden in his heart and a gambler's daring— Who knows?
She shrugs her shoulders.
Too late, Deborah.

JOEL

I said, Mother, that the Company is faced with ruin.

GADSBY

In his letters Henry suggests certain steps should be taken which, if they can be successfully negotiated, may save the firm.

DEBORAH
Indifferently.
Then you have only to take the steps, Nicholas.

GADSBY

They can be taken only with your consent, since Henry's will bequeathes the Company jointly to you and Joel. I may add that Joel has already given his consent.

JOEL

I consider it my duty to Father's memory.

DEBORAH

If you only knew, Joel, how many times I wish to pinch you to discover if you're stuffed!

JOEL
With cold indifference.
I have long realized I bore you, Mother. You will doubtless find
Simon more congenial.

DEBORAH
Stiffens. Her face becomes as hard and cold as Joel's.
Pray, what has your brother to do with this?

GADSBY
Simon has everything to do with it.

DEBORAH
I forbid you to bring his name into this discussion. I have forgotten
him.

GADSBY
Deborah, for the sake of the Company—

DEBORAH
I care nothing for the Company!

JOEL
You will have to sell this home. You will have nothing. What
will you do? Go and beg Simon and his wife to let you live on
charity with them?

DEBORAH
I would rather beg in the gutter—!

JOEL
Of course, you may always have a home with me. But on a bookkeeper's wage—

DEBORAH
Can you possibly imagine—?

JOEL
No. So I advise you to listen to Mr. Gadsby, as he requests.

GADSBY
Your position is—er—precarious, unless— What Henry suggested
is this: He realized that Joel has not had the requisite executive
experience to take control under such difficult circumstances.

JOEL

Father knew I have not the ability to be head of the Company under any circumstances.

DEBORAH

Stares at him wonderingly—slowly.
There are times when I almost respect you, Joel.

GADSBY

Humm. Henry appears to have had complete confidence in Simon's ability. He seems to have carefully followed Simon's career.

JOEL

I know that because the reports were made through me. Father did not wish to appear in the matter.

DEBORAH

Poor Joel. Your father never had time to spare others' feelings.

JOEL

I dislike pity, Mother.

GADSBY

Henry's suggestion is that you and Joel approach Simon—

DEBORAH

Go begging to Simon? I did that once—

GADSBY

What Henry recommended is a straight business deal, which will be equally to Simon's advantage and yours. He knew that Simon's business is still a small local affair—nothing to compare to the Harford Company. To be its head is to be a leading figure in commerce, as Simon, who once worked under his father and knows the business, will be the first to appreciate.

DEBORAH

So I am to ask Simon to accept the leadership of the Company, is that it?

GADSBY

Yes. A controlling interest. That is only just if he saves it from ruin. And Henry believed he has the means to save it. He has been shrewd enough to anticipate conditions and foresee the panic and ruin which is gathering around us.

He hesitates—then uncomfortably.

Humm— Of course, Henry foresaw that there might be difficult personal aspects. He knew that Simon still feels a resentment—

DEBORAH

If we are facing facts, let us face them. Simon hated him.

GADSBY

But Henry evidently believed that you and Simon still—

JOEL

Simon will not wish you to be ruined, Mother.

DEBORAH

So I am cast in the role of chief beggar! Henry must have lost his famous shrewdness in more ways than one. He fails to consider the one person who can laugh at his calculations, and who will take great pleasure in doing so—Simon's wife! If you think she will ever consent— Oh no, you will find she has never forgiven Henry for humiliating her pride.

GADSBY

Henry knew that. He—er—evidently relied on your tact and diplomacy, Deborah, to convince her.

DEBORAH

I? She hates me!

GADSBY

One further thing Henry suggested, to make his proposal as equitable as possible for Simon and his—er—family. He thought, as they would have to sell their present home and come to the city, and as this home is much too large for you and Joel, that—

DEBORAH

That I should invite that vulgar Irish biddy and her brats to live with me!

With almost a gloating smile.

Yes, that would be a greater opportunity than I had ever hoped—

35

Then resisting more violently than before—furiously.
No! How dare you make such a shameless proposal!

JOEL

It is Father who proposes it, Mother.

DEBORAH

And I hoped I had at last escaped the dunning of wifely duty! For the love of God, hasn't his death even that meaning?

JOEL

We are waiting for your consent, Mother.

DEBORAH

What an implacable bill-collector you would make, Joel.
Violently.
No, I will not have it! What have I to do with the Company? Let it be ruined! Do you think I fear poverty?

GADSBY

Humm! As your attorney, Deborah, I strongly advise you to consent.

DEBORAH

Rising to her feet.
No! I tell you I swore to myself years ago I would never involve myself in such a low intrigue! And I still desired life then. Do you think you can tempt me now when I am an ugly, resigned old woman whose life is only in the mind? You are wasting your time, gentlemen.
She makes a gesture of arrogant dismissal.

JOEL

With cold condemnation.
How long are you going to keep us waiting here on your perverse whims? I have always disliked this garden.
He stares around him with dislike.
Nothing is natural, not even Nature.

GADSBY

Staring around him in turn—as if fighting against an influence.

Yes, Deborah, the atmosphere is hardly conducive to—common sense, shall I say?

Then haltingly, as if the influence took hold on him, staring at her.

My dear Deborah. Why should you talk of being old? Ridiculous! You ugly? You are beautiful!

Instinctively her face lights up with an eager grateful smile.

Why, you could be the most wooed widow in the city! I myself would jump at the chance—

Deborah gives a soft, gratified little laugh. He goes on hastily.

Not that there ever was a chance—I know that. Besides, this is hardly the time to speak of— You will forgive me, Joel. Your father always permitted me a little harmless gallantry. He knew your mother could never take a short, fat man seriously. Nor could any other woman. Of course, there was Napoleon. But I admit I am no Napoleon, although at times I have dreamed—

Abruptly wrenching his eyes from hers—grumbles irritably to himself.

Humph! What rubbishy thoughts for a man of my years and profession! Her eyes always did make a fool of me.

Reacts—with an extreme professional portentousness.

I must protest against your acting so childishly, Deborah. You know there is one honorable course to take. As a woman of breeding and honor, you have no possible choice.

DEBORAH

With an undercurrent of tense eagerness.

Yes, I suppose it is my duty to see it only in that light. And then there is no choice, is there? It is fate!

With a strange frightened urgency.

But you must bear witness, won't you, Nicholas, that I fought against this opportunity, that I did not desire it and did all in my power to reject it?

JOEL

You consent?

DEBORAH

Slowly—as if forcing the words out in spite of herself.

Yes. I consent. Ah! I feel tempted to live in life again—and I am afraid!

JOEL

It's settled, then. We will go and see Simon tomorrow. I shall arrange for places in the stage.

He bows with cold courtesy to his mother.

Good night, Mother. Are you coming, Gadsby?

GADSBY

Yes, Joel.

He starts to go with Joel—then stops, after a glance at Deborah.

Go on. I'll follow in a moment.

Joel goes. Deborah is staring before her. Gadsby coughs embarrassedly.

Upon my soul, Deborah, I—er—I cannot see what there is to be apprehensive about in your consenting to the one sensible course.

DEBORAH

I am afraid of myself, Nicholas.

GADSBY

Stuff and nonsense! It will distract your mind and give you a new interest in life.

DEBORAH

Ah, if it only could be a new interest, Nicholas, and not an old one risen from my dead. With what joy I would welcome it, then! With what humble gratitude would I give thankfulness to God for the undreamed-of miracle! Oh, if you knew how I have prayed for resurrection from the death in myself!

GADSBY

I—I do not understand you.

DEBORAH

Forcing a smile—contemptuous and at the same time affectionate.

No, that is why I can safely tell you all my secrets, Nicholas.

38

GADSBY

I remember how devoted you once were to Simon. You may even find you can like his wife, when you know her. Forgetting prejudice, you must admit she has been an estimable wife and mother. Oh, I expect you to storm at me for pleading her case—

DEBORAH

I will not storm. I understand her feeling toward me. In her place, I would feel the same.

She smiles wryly.

There. You see how just I am.

GADSBY

Eagerly.

I do, indeed! But I was thinking most of your grandchildren—the opportunity they present to you. You can have no feeling against them, nor blame them in any way for the past. Your blood is in them. Children in this garden—

DEBORAH

Yes, I do see, Nicholas. Like an amazing revelation—a miraculous hope that would never have occurred to me if you hadn't— It could be the chance for a new life—escape from the death within myself. Resign myself to be a grandmother! You astonish me, Nicholas. I have heard of wisdom from babes, but who could dream of it from a bachelor! I really believe you are trying to make a good woman of me, Nicholas!

She laughs softly—then quickly, seeing he is hurt.

No. Forgive my teasing. I am truly grateful. If you could know how grateful! And I swear to you I will try. It will not be easy. You do not know how bitterly Sara suspects me. Or how well she understands—what I was. It will be difficult to convince her of my good motives, and persuade her to trust me with her children. I shall have to be very cunning. I must be very meek and humble.

Suddenly, angry at herself.

No! I talk as if I were planning to pretend and play a part! But I *am* meek now! I *am* humble! I am willing to beg her on my knees to give me this chance to be reborn! I can love her for it if she does! Because if she can trust me, I can learn to trust myself again!

39

I can make her love me and her children love me! I can love again!
Oh, I may surprise myself, I think, with my undreamed-of talents
as a good woman! Already at the mere prospect of escape, I feel
a rebirth stirring in me! I feel free!

GADSBY

Good! Excellent! I am delighted you—

DEBORAH

And to prove my escape—as a symbol— Watch and bear witness,
Nicholas! I will cast out my devil, the old Deborah—drag her
from her sneering-place in my mind and heart, and push her back
where she belongs—in there—in perpetual darkness.
She advances up the steps—with a final push.
"Depart from me, ye cursed!"
She grabs the doorknob, shutting the door.
And shut the door! Lock it!
She does so.
There! Now question, and sneer and laugh at your dreams, and
sleep with ugliness, and deny yourself, until at last you fall in love
with madness, and implore it to possess you, and scream in silence,
and beat on the walls until you die of starvation. That won't take
long, now you no longer have me to devour, Cannibal!

GADSBY

Come, come, Deborah. This is all most unseemly!

DEBORAH
Turns to him.
It is done! She is dead to me. Sshh! Do you hear, Nicholas?

GADSBY

Hear what?

DEBORAH

The footsteps beyond the wall. They have stopped receding. I
think Life remembers he had forgotten me and is turning back.
*Suddenly she is conscious of the expression on Gadsby's
face and she bursts into natural teasing laughter.*
Heavens, Nicholas! What an alarmed face! Did you think it was
a burglar I heard?

GADSBY

God bless me! Who could know what to think? Life, indeed!
What fantastic rubbish, Deborah!

CURTAIN

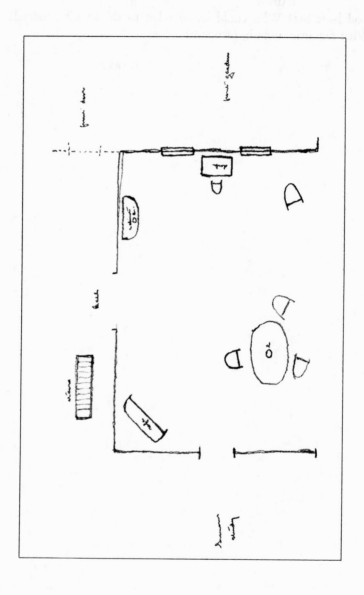

Act One, Scene Three

Scene   *Sitting-room of Sara Harford's home in a textile-mill town about forty miles from the city. The following night. The room is small, a typical room of the period, furnished without noticeable good or bad taste. The atmosphere is one of comfort and a moderate prosperity. At front, to the left of center, is a table with a lamp and three chairs. In the middle of the left wall is a closed door leading into Simon's study. In the left corner, rear, is a sofa. The doorway to the entrance hall—and the stairs to the second floor—is in the middle of the rear wall. At right of this doorway is a cabinet with a lamp. There are two windows in the right wall, looking out on the front garden and the street. Between the windows is a desk with a chair. At right-front is a big armchair.*

As the curtain rises, from the hall at rear the sound of small boys' arguing voices is heard coming down the stairwell from the floor above. Then Sara's voice trying to quiet them and, for the moment, succeeding. In this pause, the door at left is opened and SIMON enters. Physically, he appears to have changed no more than one would normally expect. His spare frame has put on ten pounds or so, but it still has the same general effect of loose-jointed, big-boned leanness. His large-featured Yankee face looks his thirty-one years. But there is a noticeable change in the impression his personality projects—a quality of nervous tension, the mental strain of a man who has been working too hard and puts unrelieved pressure on himself. As he comes into the room, he is frowning, his eyes preoccupied. He comes to the table and stands staring down at it preoccupiedly. He is startled by a hubbub from the floor above, a chorus of boys' excited voices, the sound of scuffling coming through the ceiling, followed by a resounding thump and a chorus of laughter. His face lights up. He smiles and chuckles to himself.

Then Sara's voice is heard in a commanding tone, and the uproar subsides obediently. Simon sits in the chair at left-front of table. He picks up two folded newspapers from the table, puts one paper aside, starts to open the other, hesitates, then determinedly opens it. His eyes fix on one story. As he reads it, his face becomes hard and bitter. Finished, he lowers the paper to his lap and stares over it. He hears Sara coming down the stairs in the hall and at once represses his thoughts and looks back toward the doorway at rear smilingly.

SARA enters at rear. She is flushed, her hair disarranged on one side, her eyes laughing and fondly maternal. She exudes an atmosphere of self-confident loving happiness and contentment. She is much better looking than she had been in her pregnancy. Her figure is buxom, but beautifully proportioned, with full breasts and a slender waist.

SIMON
Rising as she enters—smilingly.
Well! What's been going on up there?

SARA
We had a pillow fight.
She laughs—then suddenly shamefaced.
But what a way for me—and you in your study trying to write!
She kisses him impulsively.

SIMON
I couldn't get interested in it tonight, anyway.
He looks away from her. She sits in the chair at right-front, and he sits where he had been.

SARA
Too casually.
What paper is it you've been reading?

SIMON
Garrison's *Liberator*.

SARA

Uneasily.

Oh, I meant to hide it. I didn't want you to see—

SIMON

Why? I knew Father had died. The report of his funeral means nothing.

SARA

Resentfully.

I can't understand your Mother not inviting you to the funeral.

Bitterly.

Unless she thought I wouldn't let you go without me, and she didn't want her poor Irish relations shaming her before the notables!

SIMON

Now, now. She knew Father wouldn't have wished me to come and pretend grief for public opinion's sake. As for her having Joel write me he was dead instead of writing me herself, you know I've never had a letter from her since I saw her that time at my cabin.

SARA

She's a wise woman and knows it'd do no good for her to interfere—

SIMON

I'd hardly call the letters she once wrote me interfering.

SARA

She was always reminding you about your book.

SIMON

Stares at her—smilingly.

You objected to that? And for the last couple of years, who has been encouraging me to write it?

SARA

I have. But that's different.

She grasps his hand and presses it—tenderly possessive.

Because I love you, and you're mine, and your happiness is my happiness.

SIMON

Why, often I had forgotten all about the darned thing, but you would send me into my study to work on it like a regular slave-driver!

SARA

Laughingly.

Oh, I'm not as bad as that, Darling.

SIMON

But I've had a dark suspicion for some time. I think you calculated very cunningly the best way to convince me it was nonsense was to make me attempt it and then prove to myself—

SARA

Guiltily.

No.

SIMON

There I was at night in my study trying to convince myself of the possibility of a greedless Utopia, while all day in my office I was really getting the greatest satisfaction and sense of self-fulfillment and pride out of beating my competitors in the race for power and wealth and possessions!

He laughs, bitterly amused.

It was too absurd.

SARA

You're giving it up forever?

SIMON

I threw all I've done in the fireplace and burned it. You don't have to look so triumphant, Sara.

SARA

Guiltily.

I'm not. I— No, I won't lie. I am glad you have found it out for yourself. You know I've never believed your dream would work, with men and women what they are.

SIMON

With us as we are, for example? But you're quite right. Rousseau was simply hiding from himself in a superior, idealistic dream—as Mother has always done, in a different way. You were right to blame her, Sara. It was really her influence that made me first conceive the idea of my book. I can see that now — her haughty disdain for Father because he was naturally absorbed in his business. And yet all the time she owed everything to his business—the comfort she loved, the protected privacy, her fanciful walled-in garden, the material security which gave her the chance to remain aloof and scornful! But why think of that now? Except I thank God I freed myself in time, and then met you, who are so simply and passionately conscious of life as it is, and love it and are healthily eager and happy to be alive and get all you can from it.

Abruptly.

But all I wanted to tell you was my final decision about the book.

SARA

I'll never mention it again.

SIMON

No, all you have to do is read your daily newspaper and see what man is doing with himself. There's the book that ought to be written—a frank study of the true nature of man as he really is and not as he pretends to himself to be—a courageous facing of the truth about him—and in the end, a daring assertion that what he is, no matter how it shocks our sentimental moral and religious delusions about him, is good because it is true, and should, in a world of facts, become the foundation of a new morality which would destroy all our present hypocritical pretenses and virtuous lies about ourselves. By God, it's a fascinating idea. I've half a mind to try it!

SARA

If it isn't just like you to start dreaming a new dream the moment after you've woke up from the old! It's the touch of the poet in you!

SIMON

Nonsense! There never was any poet in me. I couldn't spare the time, for one thing. It's a difficult period for trade this country is in now. I've got to concentrate all my brains and energy on our business affairs. That mad fool, Jackson! His insane banking policy is ruining the country!

SARA

Well, he can't ruin us. We've got fifty thousand dollars, the most of it in gold English guineas. The hard times won't touch that.

SIMON

No. They will make it more valuable.

SARA

And you had the brains to see the hard times coming before anyone.

SIMON

But my competitors kept on expanding, and now it's too late, poor devils. And when the time comes we will be in a position to take advantage of others' lack of foresight. That will be our opportunity to expand. It won't take long for us to get the hundred thousand we have set as our goal. Or more.

SARA

No. That's enough. We promised ourselves—

SIMON

You don't realize what extraordinary opportunities there will be, Sara. In shipping, for example, there are many firms on the verge of bankruptcy already. Later on I know we could buy up one for comparatively nothing.

SARA

Uneasily.

No, stick to your own trade, Simon, whatever you do.

SIMON

Don't forget I had my first business training with my father's company. And we can't dismiss the shipping trade as something that doesn't concern us. Our cotton is brought to us in ships, isn't it? If we owned our own shipping company, managed as economically and efficiently as I know I could manage it, it would be of tremendous advantage to our mills— I tell you, Sara, the more I think of it, the more opportunities I foresee. Take banking.

Banks are beginning to fail right and left already, and before long
I prophesy—

SARA

Laughingly.

Stop! You have my head spinning! You'll be dreaming yourself
the King of America before you know it!

SIMON

Still, if we had that two hundred thousand in specie now—

SARA

Scolding him as though he were a small boy.

Now, now, you're too greedy. And you mustn't do so much
planning and scheming, when it's getting near bedtime, or you'll
never settle down to sleep.

SIMON

Leans back in his chair, suddenly conscious of weariness.

Yes, I am tired. But I'll sleep soundly again now I've put that
damned book out of my mind.

He closes his eyes, and then opens them to stare before him.

What a damned fool a man can make of himself. Keep on deliberately denying what he knows himself to be in fact, and encourage
a continual conflict in his mind, so that he lives split into opposites
and divided against himself! All in the name of Freedom! As if at
the end of every dream of liberty one did not find the slave, oneself, to whom oneself, the Master, is enslaved!

He chuckles bitterly.

SARA

Ah now, Darling, don't start that black loneliness—

SIMON

Throws off his mood.

Oh, I'm not. That's finished and done with. I promise not to
bewilder you with opposites ever again.

*They are interrupted by the sound of the knocker on the
front door, coming from the hall at rear.*

Now who the devil—?

He gets up and goes out, rear, frowning irritably. Sara sits

listening. From the hall Simon's voice is heard exclaiming
with astonishment, "Mother!" and Deborah's voice
"Simon." Sara springs to her feet and stands tensely
defensive, her expression frightened for a second, then
hardening into hostility. Deborah's voice again. Then
Simon's and Joel's in cold formal greeting to each other.
A moment later DEBORAH *and Simon appear in the door-*
way at rear with JOEL *behind them. Deborah wears deep*
mourning. Her face is extremely pale. Outwardly she is
all disciplined composure, the gracious, well-bred gentle-
woman, with just the correct touch of quiet resignation
in her bearing which goes with her widow's black. But
one senses an inner tense excitement, a vital eager mental
aliveness. At sight of her, Sara instantly puts on her
most ladylike manners, as if responding in kind to a
challenge.

DEBORAH
Comes forward with a gracious smile, holding out her
hand.
I am glad to see you again, Sara.

SARA
Takes her hand, smiling in return—a bit stiltedly.
It is a great pleasure, Mrs. Harford.

SIMON
This is my brother, Joel, Sara.
Joel makes her a formal bow. Sara acknowledges the
introduction in silence, then turns to Deborah.

SARA
Won't you sit down?
She indicates the chair in which she had been sitting.
Deborah takes it.
You sit there by your mother, Simon.
She goes to the armchair at right-front. Simon sits in his
old place at left-front of table. Joel takes the chair at rear
of table.

SIMON
This *is* a surprise, Mother.

DEBORAH
We arrived on the stage about an hour ago and went to the hotel to make ourselves presentable.

SIMON
You must stay with us. We have a room for you, if not for Joel—

JOEL
I should stay at the hotel in any case.

DEBORAH
No, no. I would not dream of imposing on Sara's hospitality.

SARA
We've a fine room always ready. We've had Southern planters as our guests, who are used to great mansions on their estates.
Abruptly, she is ashamed of her bragging and adds lamely.
We should feel very offended if you refused us Mrs. Harford.

DEBORAH
Why then, I accept your hospitality. It will give me an opportunity of knowing your children.
For a moment she looks into Sara's eyes with a strange, almost pleading earnestness.

SARA
I'm sure you'll like them. No one could help—
She smiles.
But of course they're mine and I'd be bound to think that.

JOEL
We must obtain Simon's decision tonight, Mother, so I can return on the first stage tomorrow.

SIMON
My decision?

DEBORAH
And Sara's decision.
To Joel.

I suggest Simon take you to his study. You can explain your mission there, and leave me to tell Sara.

SIMON
My decision on what?

DEBORAH
Certain last wishes of your father's, and a bargain he proposes.
She smiles.
I need not warn you to scrutinize it closely.

JOEL
Mother!

SIMON
Thank you for the warning.

DEBORAH
It was your father's wish that you decide this matter solely on its merits as a business opportunity. That is my wish too.

JOEL
Father's proposal is immensely to your advantage.

SIMON
Getting to his feet.
We shall see.
He starts for the study door at the left, Joel following.

SARA
Warningly.
Simon, remember—

SIMON
Turns back—reassuringly.
You know that I will make no decision without your consent.
He turns and opens the study door and bows curtly to Joel to precede him. They go inside and shut the door. There is a pause in which Deborah and Sara stare at each other. Deborah again with the strange earnest, almost pleading look. Sara suspicious, puzzled.

DEBORAH

It is a long time since our meeting at the cabin. I am sure you notice how greatly I have changed.

SARA

With a cruel revengeful satisfaction.
You look an old woman now. But I suppose you still dream you're the King of France's sweetheart!

DEBORAH

I *am* an old woman, Sara. And I have not dreamed that dream since that day. Can you believe that, Sara?

SARA

I believe you. You couldn't, remembering how he'd laughed.
Impatiently.
But it's no business of mine. And it isn't telling me why you're here or what you want of me.

DEBORAH

I came to beg charity from you, Sara.

SARA

You! To beg charity from me! Ah, what trick are you up to now?

DEBORAH

No. There is no trick now, Sara. I have come to beg—

SARA

Lapsing into broad brogue.
You, the great lady Harford! Glory be to God, if my father could have lived to see this day!

DEBORAH

There is only one possible chance for me to live again, Sara, and only you can give it to me.

SARA

I'm buying no pig in a poke.

DEBORAH

I want the chance to be unselfish, to live in others' lives for their sake and not my sake. I want to make myself an unselfish mother and grandmother. I want even to become a loving mother-in-law who can rejoice in your happiness as my son's wife and his happiness as your husband.

> SARA

Moved—impulsively.
Ah, that's good and kind of you, Madam.
Abruptly hostile—contemptuously.
If you're not lying to play me some trick!

> DEBORAH

I feel now what I felt that day at the cabin that you and I in a way complement each other and each has something the other lacks and needs—

> SARA

If you imagine I have any need for your great lady's airs and graces, you're badly mistaken, Mrs. Harford!

> DEBORAH

Continuing as if she hadn't heard.
—that if we gave each other the chance, we could be close friends and allies.

> SARA

Are you begging me for—?
With a strange derisive satisfaction.
Indeed and you've changed entirely.
Grudgingly.
I know I don't hate you any more. I'm too sure of Simon now. And if I could trust you—

> DEBORAH

What I'm begging for above all, Sara, is the chance to find a new life. If you knew how horribly alone I have been for so long, Sara, sitting in my garden with an empty dreamless mind, with only the hope of death for company. I need to be reminded that life is not the long dying of death by the happy greedy laughter of children! Will you give me that chance, Sara?

> SARA

It's true you have nothing in life, poor woman, and how could I be so cruel and hard-hearted as to turn you away, when I'm so rich and you so poverty-stricken.

DEBORAH

Oh, thank you, Sara. It means the difference between life and death to me!

SARA

Uneasy, as if already regretting her consent.
I'm only doing it because it was through the money you loaned us when we were married we got our start.
Then suddenly suspicious.
Wait! What has this got to do with the business his brother is telling Simon?

DEBORAH

Smilingly evasive.
I'd rather not, Sara, if you don't mind. My only real interest is the chance for a new life, which you can give me whether you and Simon decline his father's offer or not.

SARA

But what is the offer? You can tell me that.

DEBORAH

Carelessly.
Why, all I understand about it is that my husband suggested that Joel and I should offer Simon a controlling interest if he would assume direction of the Company's affairs.

SARA

My husband to be head of the Harford Company?
Abruptly—then frowning.
But I don't see—

DEBORAH

The Company, I believe, is at present in need of cash—

SARA

Ah, so that's it! The gold we've slaved to save! No, thank you, Mrs. Harford. My husband has his own business, and it's enough. He don't want the Harford Company.

DEBORAH
Shrugs her shoulders indifferently.

Well, that's for you and Simon to decide. My husband proposed that I make over to you, as part of the bargain, a one-half interest in my house and garden—

SARA

The Harford mansion! It's one of the finest in the city!

DEBORAH

Yes, it is really a very beautiful and valuable property, Sara. And I need not tell you how delighted I would be. In fact I want to double my husband's offer and deed the whole property over to you. All I ask in return is that you allow me to live there with you—and my grandchildren.
She adds laughingly.

Oh, I admit this is shameless bribery on my part, Sara, but I am so alone, and it would mean so much to me—

SARA
Touched and greedy.

I think it's very generous of you, Mrs. Harford.
Then warily.

But, of course, it depends on what Simon—

DEBORAH

Oh, certainly. And now, let us not talk of business any more.
Eagerly.

Could I see my grandchildren now? Oh, I know they must be asleep. All I wish is a peek at them, so I can begin feeling myself an actual, living, breathing grandmother!
She laughs gaily.

SARA

Indeed you can.
She runs from her chair and Deborah gets up, too.

Only I better go up alone first and make sure they're asleep. If one of them was awake and saw you he'd be so excited and full of questions—

DEBORAH
Smiling.

Oh, I know. I remember Simon—
She stops abruptly, her expression suddenly bitterly resentful.

SARA

I'll be right back, Mrs. Harford.

DEBORAH
Throws off her mood—smilingly.

I would be grateful if you could call me Deborah from now on.

SARA
With instinctive humility.

No, that's too familiar—
Then hating herself for this—assertively.

All right, I will, Deborah.
She goes out, rear.

DEBORAH
Stares after her—jeeringly.

At least old age has not impaired your talent for acting, Deborah!
Then savagely.

No! You lie! You know you lie! I meant every word sincerely!
I will make myself love her! She has given me life again! I—
She stops abruptly and sits down again as the door from the study is opened and Simon enters with Joel. Joel's expression is one of cold, bitter humiliation. Simon is repressing a feeling of gloating satisfaction and excited calculation. He comes and puts a protecting, possessive hand on his mother's shoulder.

SIMON

Poor Mother.
She gives a quick bitter look up at his face and moves her shoulder away.

I think I can promise I'll soon win back for you all his stupid folly has lost.

JOEL

It is cowardly to insult the dead.

SIMON

He did act like a fool, as Mother will agree—

DEBORAH

I agree with Joel that the dead are, after all, the dead.
Simon stares at her in resentful surprise.
Am I to understand you accept your father's proposal?

SIMON

Did you think I would refuse to save you from being ruined?

DEBORAH

No, no! I told you it is my wish that there be no hypocritical
family sentiment in this bargain.

SIMON

Hypocritical, Mother?

DEBORAH

You hated him. As for you and me, we have not even corres-
ponded in years. In the meanwhile, we have both changed completely in character—

SIMON

Yes, I begin to see how completely you have changed!

DEBORAH

Anyway, I warn you frankly that I could never play the role of a
slavish loving mother convincingly again.

SIMON

I am glad you admit it was just a role.

DEBORAH

So now you must consider your father's and my proposal purely
and simply as a business deal. Accept, if it strikes you as a profitable
opportunity. I refuse to be indebted—to you—for anything.

SIMON

Very well, Mother.
He sits at the table—Joel behind it—curtly.

As I have told Joel, I will accept Father's proposal only on one condition. If you cannot agree to it, there is no more to be said.

DEBORAH

And what is the condition?

JOEL

It is preposterous, Mother—an insult to Father's memory!

SIMON

There can be no question of my giving up my prosperous business here to take up his bankrupt one. Father, in his blind vanity, over-estimated the prestige of his name. I have never needed that prestige. I do not need it now. My condition is that I absorb his Company in mine. There must be only my Company.

JOEL

Father would rather have faced ruin a thousand times—

DEBORAH

But unfortunately he left me to face it. I see, Simon, what an opportunity this is for you. I accept your condition.

JOEL

You have let him beat you down like a swindling horse-trader! He would accept unconditionally if you—

DEBORAH

I want your brother to drive the hardest bargain he can—

SIMON

Naturally you could expect no mercy in a strictly business deal, Mother. Then the matter is settled—provided, of course, Sara consents.

DEBORAH

Yes, I have talked with Sara and I think you will have no trouble convincing her.

SIMON

I know that, Mother. Sara does as I advise in these matters.

JOEL

Gets to his feet—stiffly to Simon.

59

I bid you goodnight. I shall go to the city by the morning stage and have the announcement made that you are assuming control of the Company.

SIMON

The sooner the better. Creditors may grow uneasy.

JOEL

Before I go— You will, of course, wish me to resign from my position—

SIMON

No. You are an excellent head bookkeeper, I know. Why should I? And I shall see that you are given an interest in my Company commensurate with the interest you were left in Father's Company.

JOEL

I shall engage an attorney to protect that interest.

SIMON

Attorney or no attorney, I could easily swindle you out of it, if I liked. But you are too helpless a foe. Goodnight.

JOEL

I will keep my position only because I feel it my duty to Father's memory to do all I can—for the Company will always be Father's Company in my eyes.

SIMON

I do not care a tinker's damn what it is in your eyes.

Joel stares at him, is about to say something more, then bows stiffly, and stalks out the door at rear. Simon frowns after him—then suddenly chuckles, with a change of manner toward Deborah.

God, he'll never change, will he, Mother? He isn't a man. He's a stuffed moral attitude!

DEBORAH

Unconsciously falling into the mood of their old affectionate intimacy.

Yes, haven't I always said Joel is God's most successful effort in taxidermy!

They laugh amusedly together—then stop abruptly and stare at each other.

SIMON

I must confess, Mother, I do not see why you should suddenly take such an antagonistic attitude toward me.

DEBORAH

You are wrong to think my present feeling is one of antagonism. No, my feeling is one of indifference.

SIMON

Mother!

DEBORAH

That is what Time does to us all. We forget and pass on. You have your life of a husband to live. You have your children. One must eliminate the past. Why not admit that?

SIMON

Very well. I do admit it.

DEBORAH

Good! There the past is finally buried, and we can start again and learn to become friends. I want to be the friend of Sara's husband, Simon. I want to be proud of what you are, of the great success I see before you. I am determined to live with a world that exists, Simon, and accept it as good. I have forgotten my old silly presumptuous cowardly disdain for material success. I hope to live to see you become a Napoleon of finance.

SIMON
Stares at her.
It is no lie that you have changed—incredibly.
Sara enters from the rear.

SARA

I'm sorry to keep you waiting so long, Deborah, but our talking here had wakened Jonathan and I had to get him back to sleep.
Glancing from one to the other—with a trace of suspicion.
What are you talking about? Where's Simon's brother?

DEBORAH

Simon was talking over this business—for the last time, I hope.

SIMON

Joel has just left. I'm sending him to the city by the first stage to announce that we are taking over Father's Company. Do you understand, Sara? His Company ceases to exist. We absorb it.

SARA

Ah, if my father had only lived to see—!
With sudden dismay.
Then you decided it all—without waiting to ask me!

SIMON

Because I was sure of your consent and I knew Mother had talked to you.

SARA

She was begging me—

DEBORAH

Yes, I begged Sara to forget all the bitterness in the past and allow me to become her friend. And she promised she would try.

SARA

Yes, I did. But—

SIMON

It is strange to think of you two as friends.

DEBORAH

He doesn't believe we can be, Sara.

SARA

Why can't we, I'd like to know? I've always felt grateful to her for giving us our start in life.

DEBORAH

Yes, we will prove it to him. We won't let him discourage us.

SIMON

What a stupid thing to say, Mother! You know very well nothing would please me more.

DEBORAH

Laughingly.

There, Sara. Now we have your husband's blessing.

SIMON

To get back to business: I tell you, Sara, this is exactly the chance for expansion we were hoping for. And a finer bargain than I would have dreamed possible, thanks to Mother. She insisted I consider it nothing but a business deal, and I don't mind confessing, now the deal is completed, that we will be getting something for practically nothing.

DEBORAH

Laughing.

And so am I. I had nothing and I am getting Sara's friendship and a chance to make a new start in life as a good grandmother.

She turns to Sara—eagerly.

May I go up and see my grandchildren now, Sara?

SIMON

No. You'd only wake them.

SARA

All she wants is to peek at them from the door.

DEBORAH

You can trust me not to wake them, Simon. Many a time I looked in at you and never disturbed you.

SARA

Oh, him. It's hard to get him to sleep but once he drops off you could fire a cannon and he'd never budge.

DEBORAH

Yes, that's the way he used to be when he was little.

She laughs.

I can see you have made him your eldest son, as well as your husband, Sara.

SARA

Laughingly.

Oh, he's been that from the day we married. Only don't let him hear you, Deborah. It'd offend his dignity.

She takes Deborah's arm—gently.

Come along now and see the children.

They start back, ignoring Simon, who has listened frowningly, feeling completely out of it.

SIMON

Wait!

As they turn back—injuredly.

You might at least wait until I have finished explaining about the bargain I drove, Sara.

SARA

Much good it will do me to listen now after you've gone ahead and agreed without consulting me at all!

SIMON

You know very well my asking your consent has never been any-thing but a formality. What do you really know of business? It is I alone who have the right—

SARA

Suddenly frightened and hurt.

Simon! You've never said that before! You—

SIMON

I'm sorry, Sara. But nothing is signed yet. I can still back out, if you wish.

DEBORAH

Can't you see, Sara, all he wants is to prove to you how clever he has been for your sake, and have you say you're proud of him.

SARA

Smiling.

I'm all the time telling him how proud I am, and making him vain and spoiling him! So go on now and tell me, Darling.

SIMON

Made self-conscious and ill at ease.

What I wanted to say is—

64

Suddenly he stares at his mother—sneeringly.

You a doting old grandmother, Mother? You've never cared about children, except as toys to play with—unless my memory is all wrong!

DEBORAH

He doesn't want to believe that I have changed, Sara.

SIMON

Oh, I'm open to proof.

SARA

Ah now, you shouldn't sneer at your mother like that. What do you know of women?

DEBORAH

I am absolutely sure now we can become great friends.

SARA

What is it you were going to say about the bargain, Simon? Maybe you don't know or you couldn't act so unfriendly toward her, that your mother is going to deed over her fine mansion and land in the city to us? She'll only live there as our guest and I'll have the whole management and be the mistress.

SIMON

I will not consent to that.

SARA
Defiantly.

But I have consented, and it's only fair you leave me to decide about our home, if you want me to agree with what you've decided about the Company.

SIMON

I told Joel I did not want even the one-half interest in Mother's home that Father suggested she offer me. We will rent a house first, and later buy our own home. We need be under no obligation to Mother—

DEBORAH

I told you there could be no question of obligations. I made the offer to Sara as part of my bargain with her, and, to be frank, I think I am getting all the best of it. I will still have all the privileges of my home and none of the responsibilities of actual ownership. And I will have Sara and my grandchildren for company. No, if there is any obligation, I am obliged to Sara.

SARA

No, Deborah, it's a great bargain for us, too. Can't you see, Simon, that we'll be getting a fine mansion for nothing at all, with a beautiful, spacious garden for the children to play in?

DEBORAH

Really, Sara, your husband's attitude is most unflattering. You would think I was some wicked old witch, the way he dreads the thought of living in the same house with me!

SIMON

Don't be silly, Mother. I—

DEBORAH

He seems to feel so antagonistic to me because I didn't answer a few letters. But I know you appreciate my reasons for that, Sara.

SARA

I do, and I'm grateful you had the fairness and good sense not to—

SIMON

So it is I who am antagonistic, Mother? Well, perhaps I am—now—with good reason—but if I am, whose wish was it—?

Then abruptly, with cold curtness, shrugging his shoulders.

But, as you said, Sara, our home should be your business, and I am willing to abide by your decision. I shall have to concentrate all my attention on reorganizing my Company.

Eagerly.

You can't realize what an opportunity this is for me, Sara, and what a tremendous bargain I have got! Father became panic-stricken the minute he found himself out of his conservative depth. He greatly exaggerated the danger. It will be easy for me—

DEBORAH

Let's leave our Napoleon to his ambitious destiny and go up to the children, Sara.

SARA

He'll be owning the whole world in his mind before you know it.
They turn towards the door at rear, laughingly.

SIMON

Wait! Sara, I would like to utter a word of warning—in Mother's
presence. I do not possess the entire confidence in this sudden
friendship between you you both appear to have. It will be a
difficult matter when two such opposites as you are have to live
together in the same home day after day, with continual friction
and conflict of character developing. And remember I have the
right to expect a peaceful atmosphere in my home. I will have too
many important things on my mind to be distracted by domestic
dissensions. So please don't come to me—

DEBORAH

Gaily—but with a strange undercurrent.
I hereby take a solemn oath never to come to you.

SARA

What's come over you, Darling? It isn't like you to act so grudging
and stubborn—

DEBORAH

Yes, one would think he preferred us to be jealous enemies—

SIMON

You know very well, and Sara knows, it has always been my
dearest hope that you should know and love each other. I made
the objection I did only because I wanted to convince myself you
were sure of each other's good faith. It needed only your recon-
ciliation to complete my happiness and give me absolute confidence in the future.

*He kisses them. Sara's face lights up happily. Deborah's
remains teasingly mocking.*

CURTAIN

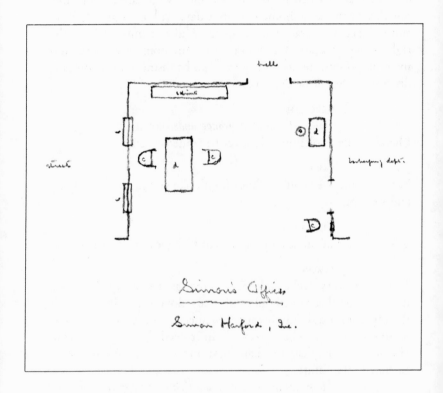

Simon's Office

Simon Harford, Inc.

Act Two, Scene One

Scene   *Simon's private office in the offices of Simon Harford Inc. It is late Summer, 1840.*

The room is small, well-proportioned, panelled in dark wood. The furniture is old, heavy and conservative. A dark rug is on the floor of polished oak boards. On the walls are pictures of Washington, Hamilton, Daniel Webster, and, incongruously, John C. Calhoun. In the left wall are two windows looking out on the street. Between the windows is a chair. Before the chair, Simon's desk, with another chair on the other side of it. In the rear wall right is a door leading into the hall. At left of this door, a tall cabinet stands against the wall. At right-front is a door leading into the bookkeeper's office. Farther back against the wall is a high desk with a tall stool in front of it. At front-right is another chair.

As the curtain rises, SIMON *enters at rear and comes to his table. He has changed greatly in the four years and looks older than the thirty-five he is. His body has put on twenty pounds or more of solid flesh, mostly around his chest and shoulders and arms, which gives him a formidably powerful appearance, but there is also a suggestion of paunch. His face has become thinner, more heavily lined and gaunt and angular. There are patches of grey over his temples. His expression is that of one habitually tense. His manner is curtly dictatorial. He speaks rapidly and incisively. He is dressed conservatively in dark clothes, obviously expensive. He wears them well but indifferently, as becoming to his position and not himself.*

He sits down, picks up the morning mail stacked on his desk, and at once becomes concentrated on going through it. The manner in which he does this is characteristic. He

*goes from one letter to the next with astonishing rapidity,
seeming to take in the contents of each at a glance and
make an instant decision, setting it on the table at his
right, or dropping it in the wastebasket.*

The door at right is opened and JOEL HARFORD *enters,
closing the door quietly behind him. He stops to glance
at his brother, then comes and stands in front of his desk.
Joel looks older. The stoop in his shoulders is more
pronounced, with a suggestion of weariness and resignation now beneath the uncompromising rigidity of his
habitual poise. He stands waiting. Simon deliberately
ignores his presence—or attempts to, but it immediately
gets on his nerves, and at last he exclaims exasperatedly.*

SIMON

Well? Is this another of your periodical duty-to-the-Company
protests against my management? If so, I don't care to listen.

JOEL

As a stockholder, it is my right—

SIMON

Your right has no power. So you have no right. But relieve your
conscience, if you must. You can have the stupid effrontery to
criticize my leadership in the face of all I've accomplished in four
years! I have five mills now, all running profitably, instead of
one. I have transformed what was Father's bankrupt business into
a marine division of my Company which is a model of its kind.
I have—

JOEL

Interrupts coldly.

You pay off debts only in order to borrow more largely. You go
on gambling—

SIMON

Don't be a frightened old woman! It is not gambling when I
know the dice are loaded in my favor.

JOEL

I refer now to the deal for the railroad you are to conclude this morning. You know nothing of railroading.

SIMON

I *will* know all there is to know.

JOEL

Finally, I want to warn you again against the growing unscrupulousness with which you take advantage of other's misfortunes. You are making the Company feared and hated.

SIMON

I want it to be feared. As for others, I do to them as they would do to me—if they could! I ask no quarter. Why should they? What a sentimental ass you are, Joel! The only moral law here is the strong are rewarded, the weak are punished. All else is an idealistic lie—a lie that I would be stupid to permit to get in my way, or in my Company's way.

JOEL

I am thinking of Father's Company, not of you. But I am wasting words.

He turns toward the door to right.

I will go back to my work.

SIMON

Yes, for God's sake!

Then as Joel goes toward the door, he speaks in a conciliating tone.

Wait! Sit down a while.

He indicates the chair at right of his desk. As Joel stares in cold surprise without making any move, he bursts out angrily.

I said sit down! Either you obey me or you look for another job!

Joel's face betrays no emotion. He comes back and sits down stiffly in the chair.

I'm sorry, Joel. It has been a strain getting this affair of the railroad settled.

He pauses, then goes on. Gradually his eyes drop from

Joel to his desk, and more and more it seems he is talking to himself.

I concentrate all my mind and energy to get a thing done. I live with it, think of nothing else, eat with it, take it to bed with me, sleep with it, dream of it—and then suddenly one day it is accomplished—finished, dead!—and I become empty, but at the same time restless and aimless, as if I had lost my meaning to myself. A vacation would be in order at such times. But where? How? A voyage to France, say—with Sara—a second honeymoon. But Sara would not leave the children, and to take the children along would mean it would be their vacation with their mother, not mine with my wife. Perhaps Sara would even insist on taking Mother with us! They have grown to be such loving friends, drawn to each other by their devotion to the children! I assure you, I am left entirely out of it now. That is Mother's doing, of course. She imagines she has been very subtle, that I have not seen. But I have promised myself that as soon as I had time, I would put a stop to her greedy scheming, and now the railroad deal is completed—

He smiles strangely.

That may be the change in activity I need.

He pauses.

If you ever fall in love, Joel, take my advice and do not marry. Keep your love your mistress with no right of ownership except what she earns day by day, what she can make you pay for possession. Love should be a deal forever incomplete, never finally settled, with each party continually raising the bids, but neither one concluding a final role.

He laughs mockingly at Joel's cold disapproval.

Yes, my advice to you would be to shun marriage and keep a whore instead!

SIMON

JOEL

I cannot see why you wish to discuss such matters with me.

SIMON

No, neither can I—except that I can trust you to listen without hearing much.

With a conciliating manner.
Why is it you never come to visit Mother?

SIMON

JOEL
You know she has as little desire to see me as I have to see her.

SIMON
You would be astounded at the way she has transformed herself.
It is as though she had slowly taken possession of Sara in order
to make of my wife a second self through which she could live
again. Or, in another aspect, trick Sara into being an accessory in
the murder of that old self, which was once my mother. And so
leave me motherless. But at the same time by becoming Sara,
leave me wifeless, for naturally I could not regard—
*He stops abruptly—then goes on with an increasing
brooding strangeness.*
Sometimes the two have appeared to lose their separate identities
in my mind's eye—have seemed, through the subtle power of
Mother's fantastic will, to merge and become one woman—a
spirit of Woman made flesh and flesh of her made spirit, mother
and wife in one—to whom I was never anything more than a
necessary adjunct of a means to motherhood—a son in one case,
a husband in the other—but now no longer needed since the
mother by becoming the wife has my four sons to substitute for
me, and the wife having them, no longer needs a husband to use
in begetting— And so I am left alone, an unwanted son, a discarded lover, an outcast without meaning or function in my own
home but pleasantly tolerated in memory of old service and as a
domestic slave whose greed can be used to bring in money to
support Woman!
With vindictive calculation.
Yes, that is what Mother flatters herself she has accomplished. But
she doesn't realize there are fundamental weaknesses in her plan,
that the past is never dead as long as we live because all we are is
the past. She is going to discover, beginning today, and Sara, too,
that whenever I wish, I take back what belongs to me, no matter—
He checks himself with a sudden wary glance at Joel.
But all these fanciful speculations are nonsense.

JOEL

Gets up from his chair.

If you have done, may I go back to my work?

SIMON

Yes. Take your idiotic conscience to hell out of here!

Joel turns and goes into the bookkeeper's office at right, closing the door behind him.

Even that dull fool realized I was really addressing myself—because I have no one but myself. Yes, Mother has left me with no life but this one which she always despised—the ambition to be a Napoleon among traders! I, who once dreamed—! Rubbish! The possession of power is the only freedom, and your pretended disgust with it is a lie. You must allow for your present state of mind—the reaction of emptiness after success—you've always felt it—but never so strongly before— There is a finality in this—as if some long patient tension had snapped—as if I no longer had the power to discipline my will to keep myself united—another self rebels—secedes—as if at last I must become two selves from now on—division and confusion—a war—a duel to the death—

With revengeful bitterness.

Well, let those who are responsible for the challenge beware, for I will make it their duel, too! Yes, Mother and Sara, henceforth I must demand that each of you takes upon herself her full responsibility for what I have become. Bah! What rubbishy fantasies!— As if I really desired two damned possessive women prying and interfering in my private business! All I know is that on an impulse I asked Sara to come here—some confused feeling that if I get her alone away from Mother's influence, I would desire her again. Hadn't I better think out more exactly how I shall attack?—No, wait until you feel her out and see how much of the old greedy Sara still lies behind her present self—the ambitious Sara who used to long to own an Irish-castle-in-Spain, gentleman's estate!— who was willing to use any means—even her beautiful body—to get what she wanted. I should have swindled her into giving herself by promising marriage—and then having had all I wanted of her, deserted her—it would have served her right to be beaten at her own game—I would have forgotten her and returned to Mother, waiting for me in her garden—

74

Bitterly.

But she wasn't waiting—She was just as ruthless and unscrupulous about discarding you as Sara was in taking you. Mother took pains to point it out to me by implication that day she deliberately made up the fairy tale about the exiled Prince and the magic door—

> *He sits staring before him, frowningly concentrated, and his face sets into a mask of calculating ruthlessness. The door from the hall at rear is opened and* SARA *enters. She has not changed much in the five years. Has grown a little more matronly, perhaps, but seems no older. Is still exceedingly pretty, strong and healthy, with the same firm, pronouncedly female figure. But she is dressed much better, with discriminating taste and style now, and expensively. Her manner has taken on a lot of Deborah's well-bred, self-assured poise, and her way of speaking copies Deborah, although the rhythm of Irish speech still underlies it. She stands looking at Simon but he is oblivious of her presence. She smiles assuredly, a smile that has lost its old passionate tenderness and become entirely maternal, complacent in possessiveness—a smile that takes its proprietorship for granted. With growing amusement, she tiptoes forward until she stands by his table.*

SARA

You might ask me to sit down, Simon.

> *He jumps startledly in his chair.*

SIMON

What do you mean by sneaking—! Oh, it's you.

SARA

That's a nice greeting, after you begged me to come.

SIMON

I apologize, Sara. For a moment, I didn't recognize who it was.

> *He springs to his feet, indicating the chair across the table.*

Sit down, do.

> *She sits down and he sits down again.*

SARA

I had no idea you'd gotten so nervous.

SIMON

You have been too occupied with family affairs to notice!

SARA

Smiling.

If that isn't like you, to put the blame on me, when it's you who come home every night with your head so full of business you might as well be on the moon. Speaking of business, tell me about the Company. You never mention it any more to us at home, but everyone tells us you're becoming the young Napoleon of trade here in the city.

SIMON

Here's a bit of news you haven't heard yet, Sara. I've got the railroad now. You remember I promised myself I would. Well, it's mine!

SARA

With a forced enthusiasm.

Isn't that fine! I congratulate you, Simon.

SIMON

I have a final meeting with the directors this morning. Not very easy terms for them to accept, but they had no choice. They were on the verge of bankruptcy. I have learned from their mistakes. I'll make no mistakes!

SARA

I'm sure you won't.

SIMON

You're not very enthusiastic.

SARA

Oh, I am. But you used to say "us" and "ours."

SIMON

Ah, you feel that?

SARA

No. God knows I've as happy a life as a woman could wish with Deborah and my children.

SIMON

Yes, one should never complain of the price one must pay for what one wants from life—or thinks one wants.

SARA

I know what I want, and I have it.

SIMON

I might complain that you used to speak of our home and our children, while now—

SARA

Ah, you feel that?

SIMON

I always have the feeling at home that, although Mother has relinquished all outward show of ownership and authority, she has managed to keep in possession.

SARA

I have the only say about everything, and she's happy to let me have it.

SIMON
Smiling.

Mother has always had a subtle talent for contriving it so that others must desire what she desires—and then generously giving them their way!

SARA

I'm not such a fool—

SIMON

Not when you're on your guard.

SARA

There's nothing to suspect! And she's been such a good grandmother to the children—even if she does spoil them.

SIMON

Gives her a sharp, calculating glance—quickly.

Yes, she is spoiling them. There's no doubt about that.

SARA

And there's no harm.

SIMON

If you're sure you haven't let it go too far.

SARA

Almost angrily.

I can take care of my children, thank you— Is that your reason for inviting me here—to try and make trouble between your mother and me?

SIMON

Don't be ridiculous! I'm delighted at the friendship which has developed between you. The more so because I never dared hope—

SARA

Almost tauntingly.

We know you didn't. Well, we fooled you!

SIMON

Do you imagine I'd prefer to have you at each other's throats?

SARA

No. That'd be crazy. But Simon, I know you've kept a secret grudge against her in your heart. Isn't it about time you stopped being so childish, and forgave—?

SIMON

Don't be stupid. There's nothing to forgive. Am I not always pleasant with her?

SARA

Yes, as you'd be to an acquaintance in the street!

SIMON

But what's the use of pretending we have anything in common any more? Just because she happened to bear me into the world!

Almost any fool of a woman can have a son, and every fool of a man has had a mother! It's no great achievement on either side, and all the hypocritical values we set on the relationship are mere stupidity.

SARA

That's not true! I've my four sons and I know the love I feel for them, and the love they feel for me!

SIMON

And don't tell me Mother minds my indifference. She has learned not to need me.

SARA

With a trace of vindictive satisfaction.
That's true enough. She doesn't miss you now she has the children.

SIMON

Bitterly.
Yes. As you have.

SARA

Stares at him—defiantly.
As I have, yes.
With a strange eagerness—teasingly.
Don't tell me you're jealous of the children—with me?
Forcing a smile—placatingly.
But I hope you didn't ask me here just to quarrel with me.
She gets up and comes around the table to him.

SIMON

Forgive me. This railroad deal has been a strain.

SARA

You haven't looked well for a long time.

SIMON

Then you do notice once in a while.

SARA

Your mother has seen it too.

SIMON

Indeed? And what was it you both noticed?

SARA

That you've been changing in some queer way inside you. Sometimes at night when you sit in the parlor with us, all of a sudden,
it's like a stranger staring at me. It's a frightening feeling, Simon.
I think I began to notice it around the time you started sleeping
in your own room away from me—

SIMON

Ah, that's it, eh? Your body felt swindled and it made you suspicious, I suppose, that I might have found another woman's body
that is more beautiful and desirable to mine than yours? You
probably think I must be secretly keeping some beautiful mistress
who has stolen your place in bed!

SARA

Startled and repelled.
Simon! I don't see how it could come to your mind—
She gives him a look of frightened suspicion.
Unless you've had the thought yourself—

SIMON

His face lighting up with a pleased satisfaction.
No, no. I was only joking.

SARA

Forgetting her ladylike poise.
I don't believe you! You must have had the wish—
*With a sudden fierce passion she grabs his head and turns
his face up to hers.*
Look at me! If I thought you wanted another woman—!

SIMON

*Puts his arm around her and hugs her to him, his face
triumphantly gratified—teasingly.*
Well, what would you do?

SARA

I'd kill her! And you, too! Simon! You don't deny it! Tell me—!

SIMON

Still provocatively unconvincing, hugging her again.
No, no. Of course I would never—

SARA

You don't say that as if you meant it!

Struggling to free herself.

Let me go! I don't want you hugging me when maybe you're wishing it was another—

Furious at the thought, she grabs his shoulders and shakes him fiercely.

Is it to confess that you had me come here? Are you going to ask me to set you free to be hers? You can hold your prate! I'll see her in hell first! If any woman thinks she can take you from me, she'll find I'll fight to the death!

She sits down on the arm of his chair and hugs him to her.

You're mine till death, and beyond death, and I'll never let you go, do you hear?

She kisses him passionately on the lips.

SIMON

His face happy now with confident possession and aroused desire—but still provocatively.

So you really are jealous?

SARA

Am I flesh and blood? Don't I love you more than all the world?

SIMON

Do you? I thought the children—

SARA

Ah, the children! Not that I don't love them with all my heart. But they're not my lover and husband! You come first!

SIMON

Do I? I shouldn't say from your actions for a long time—

SARA

Indignantly.

Are you trying to say I'm to blame? Why, there's nights at home when you stare as if you were wondering what was my business there. Or you converse with us so pleasant and polite, like a gentleman guest come in to spend the evening.

SIMON

Perhaps I do feel like an intruder—

SARA

I don't know how to say it, Darling, but it's as though the minute you came home I felt everything begin to change until nothing is what it seems to be, and we all get suspicious of each other.

SIMON

Even you and Mother?

SARA

Reluctantly.

Yes.

Hastily.

No, I meant it might if we weren't careful. It's like a spell that tries to come between us.

SIMON

That is strange. I thought that you both lived in a perfect unity of interests and desires now. Sometimes I become so intensely conscious of your unity that you appear as one woman to me. I cannot distinguish my wife from— It is a bewildering confusion.

SARA

Is that when you stare at us as though you hated us?

Forces a smile.

That's a queer crazy notion for you to have, Simon— But I think I know the kind of feeling you mean. I've felt myself at times—oh, only once in a while—that she'd like me to have no wish but her wish, and no life that wasn't ruled by her life.

SIMON

Watching her.

Yes, Mother has always been extremely greedy for others' lives. You have to be constantly on guard—

SARA

Defiantly.

But she knows I'm too strong—

Abruptly shamefaced.

Ah, what am I saying! It's mean and wrong of me to suspect her.

82

And don't think I don't see how you've changed the subject to her so you wouldn't have to answer me about having a mistress. Tell me you haven't, Simon! I couldn't bear—
>*She starts to sob.*

SIMON
>*Springs up and hugs her to him—passionately.*
Of course I haven't, Sweetheart! Look at me!
>*He lifts her face to his.*
I swear—!

SARA
Oh, Darling. I know I'm foolish—but I love you so!
>*She kisses him and he responds, hugging her to him with a passionate desire. She breaks away, stirred and happy, but modestly embarrassed—with a soft laugh.*
We mustn't. Supposing someone came in! It's a long time since you've kissed me—like that, Darling.

SIMON
A long time since you've given me the chance!

SARA
I like that! You'll say next it was I that wanted you to sleep alone. You don't know how you hurt me when you did that, Simon. I tried to believe your excuse that you didn't want to keep me awake when you couldn't sleep because your mind kept making plans for the Company. But I couldn't help fearing the real reason was you didn't want me.

SIMON
>*Hugs her passionately.*
You know I want you now, don't you?

SARA
Oh, here—now—yes— But at home—

SIMON
That's why I asked you to come. Because I want you to want me as you used to, but at home there is always Mother coming between us.

SARA
Frowns.
Yes, it's true you feel her always there, watching— But she doesn't mean to interfere. The trouble is you haven't noticed the change in her. You don't know the nice, kind, contented old grandmother she is now.

SIMON
Pretending to give in.
I must admit she seems sincere in her affection for your children.

SARA
Oh, she is, Simon!

SIMON
From their talk, they must spend a great deal of their time in her garden.

SARA
A shadow of resentment shows in her face.
Yes, they do. But now they'll be away at school a lot of the day.
Defensively.
It's good for them to be with her. She's a great lady and her influence—

SIMON
I remember my own experience. If I hadn't got away from her before it was too late, she'd have made me dependent upon her for life. So you can understand why I am worried. After all, they are my sons, too.

SARA
I'm so happy to know you think of them.

SIMON
We want them trained to live with reality so when the time comes they will be capable of serving our Company—Ethan as manager of our marine division, Wolfe to direct the banking branch which we will own before long, Jonathan as our railroad executive, and Honey our representative in politics.

SARA
And I thought you'd forgotten— Forgive me, Darling.

SIMON

And I am confident they will have the brains and ability—provided we don't permit Mother to poison their minds with nonsense.

SARA

Yes.

Hesitantly.

I could ask her not to—

Guiltily.

No. It would be like breaking my part of a bargain I'd made in honor to trust her.

SIMON

It was no part of the bargain that she should steal your children.

SARA

Defensively.

Ah now, that's going too far. Anyway, they know who their mother is and who they love best.

SIMON

I have the idea they are becoming as confused between you as I. I mean as I am at home. Here you are yourself, my wife, my partner—my mistress, too, I hope.

He hugs her desirously.

SARA

Responding passionately.

Don't ever dream of having another!

SIMON

Abruptly, with a business-like tone.

We've allowed things to get in a confused muddle at home. I've been too preoccupied with the Company's affairs, and you've been too busy housekeeping for Mother and acting as nurse girl while she's left free to play she's their mother to them.

SARA

With a flash of resentful anger.

Ah, I'd like to see her try—! I begin to see a lot of things I've been blind to.

SIMON

The thing you must bear in mind is that she has never been quite normal. We might as well be frank, Sara.

SARA

Uneasily.

You mean she's insane? Ah no, that's crazy, Simon. I won't let you say such wicked things. The poor woman!

SIMON

I didn't say insane. I meant she has no sense of the rights to freedom of others.

SARA

And didn't she tell me herself she'd got to the point where she didn't dare go in that summer-house of hers for fear she'd never come out again. That's crazy, isn't it?

SIMON

Strangely.

Who knows? It all depends— Do you know if she ever goes in the summer-house now?

SARA

No. The children used to plague her to open the door but she never would. Why do you ask?

SIMON

The children must be forbidden to go to her garden or her rooms in future. She can see quite enough of them when you and I are present. And you stay away from her garden, too.

SARA

I hardly ever go.

SIMON

Then you'll give orders to the children?

SARA

Yes. But who will tell her?

SIMON

Why you, of course.

SARA

She's been so good—I hate hurting her.

SIMON

Avoiding her eyes—calculatingly, with feigned reluctance.
Well, I suppose I could tell her, if you want to be spared.

SARA

Would you? But promise me you won't be cruel to her, Simon.

SIMON

Don't be foolish, Dear. I want peace in my home. I'll drop in at her garden on my way home this evening.
With a strange happy satisfied air.
There. That puts Mother in her place—back where she belongs. Let's forget her now and think only of us.
He gives her a loving, possessive hug.
As we did in the old days.

SARA

I'm only too glad to, Darling.

SIMON

I have grown very lonely, Sara.

SARA

If you knew how unhappy and ugly I've felt since you started sleeping alone—and even before that when you'd lie beside me as if I wasn't there.

SIMON

Because I never felt we were really alone—there, in Mother's house. That's why I had you come here. I want to ask you to help me create a new life—a life in which we can be lovers again.
He presses her to him passionately.

SARA

Sensually aroused—kissing his hair.
Darling! You know I'd love nothing better!

SIMON

I want the old Sara, whose beautiful body was so greedily hungry for lust and possession, whose will was as devoid of scruple, as

87

ruthlessly determined to devour and live as the spirit of life itself! The Sara who came to my room on that night long ago, with her mind made up to use her beautiful body to keep anyone from taking what she regarded as hers.

SARA

Guiltily.

Ah, don't say—

Reproachfully.

You loved me for it! So you shouldn't remember it against me.

SIMON

Against you? I desired her more than anything in life! And now I desire her to come back more than anything in life! I owe her all my success. She is the cause of the Company! Now I need her again. I want her to come back to me here, as she came to me that night, willing to gamble with the highest possible stake, all she has, to sell her dearly.

SARA

Half pleased and flattered and half guiltily defensive.

Ah, don't talk of it that way—as if I was some low street girl who came that night to sell herself. I was bound I'd have you because I loved you so much.

SIMON

Well then, I know you will be willing to become your old true self again for me.

SARA

Well, look out then. I could be her, for I love you just as much now. But maybe you'd better let her sleep. She might be bolder than ever and want more!

She kisses him—then suddenly embarrassed and shy, pushes back from him.

But what a way for me to act! Here in your office, of all places! There's a queer thing in the air here, that makes you—and I'd stayed at home so long I'd forgotten— But I don't know what I mean—

She hugs him passionately again.

Except I love you now with all of me and all my strength, and there's no one else in the world, and I'm yours and you're mine, and I don't care how shameless I am!

SIMON

Sweetheart! That fits in exactly with my plans for our future here, because the Company is you. Your nature is its nature. It derived its life from your life, which you must claim for your own again.

SARA

Darling! Tell me plainly what your plan is.

SIMON

With a brisk, business-like air now.
This: The children will be away most of the day at school from now on. You'll be free. Well, I want you to work with me here in the Company as my secretary and secret partner.

SARA

Darling! Do you really mean—?

SIMON

Then you'll do it?

SARA

Will I? It's too good to be true!
She kisses him.
Oh, you make me so happy, Darling, when you prove you want me that much!

SIMON

Wait! There's a condition. Nothing for nothing is the rule here, you know. You'll have to pay for this opportunity.

SARA

Stop teasing now and tell me. I'll do anything you want.

SIMON

What! Do you mean to tell me a virtuous wife and mother like you will agree to become my mistress?

SARA

Shocked, embarrassed, and at the same time amused and curiously fascinated and delighted.

89

So— Then I'm the mistress you were wishing for! Well, God be thanked, you weren't dreaming of any other!

SIMON

I don't know of anyone else who would be more desirable. And I can make you a most favorable offer.

SARA

That's a nice way to talk to a decent wife! But let's hear your offer. Maybe it's not enough. I value myself highly!

SIMON

I'll agree to pay with all my worldly goods. You can get the whole Company from me—that is, of course, piece by piece, as you earn it!

SARA

The whole Company to be mine!
She kisses him suddenly with passionate gratitude.
Oh, Darling, and I was so afraid I'd become ugly to you and you were sick of me.

SIMON

Then you will take the place?

SARA

You know I will.
She hides her face on his shoulder shamefacedly—then suddenly lifts it and bursts out.
I'll play any game with you you like, and it will be fun playing I'm a wicked, lustful, wanton creature and making you a slave to my beauty.

SIMON

I was afraid you might raise objections.

SARA

Objections? When you want me and I want you?

SIMON

Well, Mother won't approve of my taking you away, as well as the children.

SARA
Resentfully.
It's none of her business.

SIMON
With a strange gloating air.
Poor Mother. She will be very lonely again. I think she will welcome visits even from me.

SARA
Don't make me think of her now.
She kisses him.
All I want to think of now is that you want me again.

SIMON
Hugs her—passionately.
I have never wanted you so much! No, not even in the days before we were married! Your body is beautiful, Sweetheart!

SARA
Kisses him passionately.
Darling!
She breaks away—with a soft happy laugh.
Aren't we the shameless ones!

SIMON
Yes, you will have to learn to be shameless here. You will have to deal daily with the greedy fact of life as it really lives. You will have to strip life naked, and face it. And accept it as truth. And strip yourself naked and accept yourself as you are in the greedy mind and flesh. Then you can go on—successfully—with a clear vision—without false scruple—on to demand and take what you want—as I have done! But you will discover all this for yourself. You will be successful. You have the natural talent. And I know you will find the game I play here in the Company as fascinating a gamble as I find it!
Strangely now—as if he were talking aloud to himself.
A fascinating game—resembling love, I think a woman will find. A game of secret, cunning strategems, in which only the fools who are fated to lose reveal their true aims or motives—even to themselves. You have to become a gambler whose face is a mask.

But one grows lonely and haunted. One finally gets a sense of confusion in the meaning of the game, so that one's winnings have the semblance of losses. The adversary across the table in whose eyes one can read no betraying emotion beyond an identical lust—this familiar stranger to whom with a trustful smile one passes the cards one has marked, or the dice one has loaded, at the moment he accepts them trustfully becomes oneself.

He frowns and shakes his head.

SARA

Now, Darling, please don't be mixing everything up in my mind. I don't know what you mean by that queer talk of marked cards and loaded dice.

SIMON

Smilingly, but with a threat underneath.

Oh, you will some day. I promise you you will.

Then, as she stares at him uneasily—abruptly business-like.

Well, I think we've settled everything.

He glances at his watch.

The railroad directors will be here in a few minutes. You will start your work here tomorrow morning.

SARA

Has gotten off the arm of his chair—jokingly bobs him a curtsy.

At your service. But remember I've no experience.

SIMON

At first, all I wish you to do is sit and watch how I deal with everything. As though you were an understudy learning to play my part. As you learn, I will let you act in my stead now and then until finally you will find yourself capable of taking my place. In your spare time, when I am away, I want you to draw plans for the country estate with the great mansion you used to dream about where we are going to retire when we have enough.

He gets up and kisses her.

No price is too high for me to pay my mistress for her love, eh?

SARA

Pulling away.

I wish you wouldn't talk as if love—

SIMON

You shall have your estate. Of course, it wouldn't do to withdraw that much capital now. There is so much to be accomplished before the Company can be free and independent and self-sufficient. Meanwhile, if you get it actually planned to the last detail—

SARA

Yes! Oh, that will be fun! And I've got every bit of it clear in my mind—or I used to have—

SIMON

You can afford to make bigger, more ambitious plans now, in view of the Company's progress since you last dreamed of it.

SARA

Oh, I can always dream bigger dreams, and I'll be only too delighted to make plans. Well, I'd better go now.

She kisses him—tenderly.

Goodbye, my darling! You've made me so happy!

She breaks from his arms and opens the door.

SIMON

Wait! Mother will be curious about your visit here but don't tell her anything. I can make the meaning clearer to her, I think.

SARA

Pityingly, but at the same time scornfully.

Ah, poor woman. I'm not anxious to tell her— Well, it'll do her good! She's gotten to think she owns me!

She stops abruptly.

Ah, I ought to be ashamed! What makes me feel like that here?

She looks around the office almost frightenedly—then hastily.

I'll go now.

She goes out and closes the door.

SIMON

Looks after her and smiles strangely—ironically.

Well, that half of my domestic responsibility-sharing scheme is launched successfully.

He walks back to his desk.

Yes, that part will work itself out according to plan.

He suddenly frowns resentfully.

Plan?—What plan?—You'd think this was some intricate intrigue you were starting, whereas it is very simple—You want Sara—All right, you take her back, and that's all there is to it—As for Mother, she has interfered and carried on an intrigue to isolate you—She must be taught to confine her activities to their proper sphere—to remain back where she belongs—Very well, put her in her place this afternoon—and that will settle her half of it.

He sits down at his desk—with a strange smile of anticipation. His expression becomes relaxed and dreamy.

It will be pleasant to find myself in her garden again after all these years.

A pause. There is a knock on the door at right. At once Simon becomes the formidable, ruthless head of the Company.

Come in.

Joel enters.

JOEL

The directors are in the outer office. I thought I should pay them the courtesy of announcing them myself considering their importance.

SIMON

They had it when they had power. But I took it from them. And your courtesy is meaningless and a cruel joke which mocks at their plight. If I was one of them, I would knock you down. Tell them to come in.

Joel stares at him—then goes out.

CURTAIN

Act Two, Scene Two

Scene   Same as Scene Two of Act One, the corner of the Harford garden with the octagonal Chinese summer-house. Late afternoon sunlight from beyond the wall at right falls on the pointed roof and the upper part of the arched lacquer-red door and ivy-covered walls of the summer-house. The shrubs, clipped as before in arbitrary geometrical designs, and the trees along the brick wall at rear glow in different shades of green. The water in the small oval pool before the summer-house is still another shade of green. The garden has the same appearance as before of everything being meticulously tended and trimmed. This effect is of nature distorted and humiliated by a deliberately mocking, petulant arrogance.

DEBORAH is sitting on the steps leading up to the summer-house door, dressed all in white. She appears greatly changed from the previous act. Where she had seemed a prematurely old, middle-aged woman then, she now has the look of a surprisingly youthful grandmother. Her body and face have filled out a little. There is something of repose and contentment in her expression, something of an inner security and harmony. But her beautiful dark eyes and her smile still retain their old imaginative, ironical aloofness and detachment.

As the curtain rises, Deborah is reading from a volume of Byron's poems. Suddenly she stops, and listens to something beyond the wall at right. Her expression changes to one of alarmed surprise and she stares at the door in the wall with dread. For a moment there is a tense silence. Then there is a sharp rap of the knocker on the door. After another moment there is a louder knock and Simon's voice calls sharply: "It's I, Mother. Open the door!" A little smile of gloating scorn comes to Deborah's lips. She allows the book to slip from her hand

95

*and goes and opens the door, then sits down by the steps
again.* SIMON *comes in, closing the door after him.*

SIMON

Good evening, Mother.

DEBORAH

Coldly pleasant.

This is an unexpected pleasure, Simon.

SIMON

Evidently. Such cooling my heels before the sacred portals. I trust
I have not intruded? May I sit down?

DEBORAH

This is your property. Pray do so.

SIMON

Sara's property.

He sits on the stone bench on her left.

DEBORAH

With a trace of mockery.

But what is hers is yours.

SIMON

Yes, that is quite true. Sara has probably told you of her visit to
my office this morning.

DEBORAH

She told me before she left you had asked her to come there.

SIMON

Feigning surprise.

That I had asked her?

She glances at him sharply. He goes on carelessly.

Well, it is of no importance who asked whom. You say she has
not mentioned our interview in any way?

DEBORAH

With forced indifference.

I imagine it concerned property of yours—her name and papers you wished her to sign. She knows I would not be interested in that.

SIMON

It had nothing to do with papers. Although, of course, it did concern property. You know Sara.

DEBORAH

As if caught off guard.
Yes, you may be sure I—
She catches herself and looks at him defensively.

SIMON

I was very glad she came. It gave me a chance to talk over with her a new arrangement at the office. I find it advisable to add a private secretary to my employ.

DEBORAH

And you had to have Sara's consent for that?

SIMON

Smilingly.
You will understand why when I tell you the one person who possesses the qualifications I desire is a young and very beautiful woman.

DEBORAH

Starts—her first instinctive reaction one of vindictive satisfaction and gloating pity.
Ah! Poor Sara! So this is what your great romantic love comes to in the end! I always knew—
Abruptly and guiltily her reaction changes to one of over-stressed moral indignation.
How dare you mention such filth to your mother! Have you become so utterly coarse that you feel no shame but actually boast you are deliberately planning to dishonor yourself and your family? But I don't know why I should be surprised. After all, this is an inevitable step in the corruption of your character that I have had to watch for years, until I could hardly recognize my son in the unscrupulous greedy trader, whose one dream was material gain!

SIMON

May I point out that you have been jumping too eagerly to conclusions, Mother? I have not said my secretary was to be anything more intimate than my secretary.

Deborah looks guilty and discomfited. He adds with a mocking smile.

I am afraid the good grandmother you have become has not entirely forgotten the French eighteenth-century memoirs in which she once lived.

DEBORAH

Stares at him strickenly—pleadingly.

Simon! It is not kind to make me remember—

With dread.

Oh, why did you come here? What—?

SIMON

And I don't see how you can think Sara would ever consent—unless you secretly believe her true nature is so greedy that she would sell anything if offered the right price.

DEBORAH

No! How dare you—! I will not have you put such thoughts in my mind about a woman to whom I owe an eternal debt of gratitude, who is the sweetest, kindest, most generous-hearted—

SIMON

I am sorry to have to disillusion you, Mother, but I think you will discover before our interview is over that Sara has not been as blind as you hoped, nor as unsuspectingly trustful.

Deborah starts and stares at him uneasily.

It does not do to hold one's enemy in the battle for supremacy in too much contempt—

DEBORAH

As though Sara and I were engaged in some fantastic duel! I bitterly resent your intruding here and attempting to create suspicion and jealousy between Sara and me. I trust her and I know she trusts me!

SIMON

We will deal with the facts, if you please, Mother, not with sentimental posing.

DEBORAH

Staring at him with a fascinated dread—stammers.

Simon! What are you trying to do? I know this is some insane plot to revenge yourself on me!

SIMON

Revenge for what? It was I who long ago, of my own free will, freed myself from your influence.

DEBORAH

With a little smile—carelessly.

So you have never forgotten that old quarrel? I remember now I used to be of the opinion it was I who forced you out into your own life. So that I might be free.

SIMON

Yes, you consoled your pride with that lie.

DEBORAH

If you wish. I appreciate that a Napoleon of affairs must believe implicitly in his own star.

She laughs softly—teasingly.

You are still such a strange, greedy boy, do you know it?

SIMON

Glancing around the garden—with a tone of nostalgic yearning.

I had forgotten the quiet and the peace here. Nothing has changed. The past is the present.

Suddenly he turns on her—harshly accusing.

You are the one jarring discordant note. The garden of your old self disowns the doting old Granny you have made yourself pretend to be.

DEBORAH

With a soft teasing laugh.

Don't tell me you are jealous of your children, too!

99

SIMON

Too? Beyond observing your obvious campaign to obtain control of the children, and pitying Sara for what I mistakenly thought was her blind trustfulness, I have regarded the matter as none of my business.

DEBORAH

Checks herself—quietly casual.

Speaking of business, you must be becoming richer and more powerful all the time.

SIMON

I concluded a deal today which adds a railroad to the Company's properties.

DEBORAH

Flatteringly but with underlying sarcasm.

My congratulations, Dear.

SIMON

Thank you, Mother. It has significance as a link in the chain in which my ships bring cotton to my mills to be made into my cloth and shipped on my railroad. But there is a lot to be done before the chain is complete.

DEBORAH

With a little mocking smile.

Yes, I perceive it is not enough.

SIMON

Deadly serious.

Far from it. The next step must be to acquire my own bank. Then I can manipulate all the Company's financing.

DEBORAH

And you will want your own stores here in the city to sell your goods.

SIMON

Yes. I have that in mind.

DEBORAH

And at the other end of your chain you should possess plantations in the South and own your own slaves, imported in your own slave ships.

SIMON
Staring before him, tense and concentrated.
Yes. Of course. I had not considered that but it is obviously the logical final step at that end. You are wonderfully shrewd and far-sighted, Mother, for a beautiful lady who has always affected a superior disdain for greedy traders like my father and me.

DEBORAH
You find me still a little beautiful? I fear you are merely flattering a poor ugly old woman.

SIMON
I am glad to find you changed in one respect, Mother. You now have the courage to face some of the things that have reality. Father had scruples. He disguised his greed with Sabbath potions of God-fearing unction at the First Congregationalist Church. I fear no God but myself! I will let nothing stand between me and my goal!

DEBORAH
What goal, Simon?

SIMON
Turns to her in surprise.
But I thought you saw that, Mother. To make the Company entirely self-sufficient. It must attain the all-embracing security of complete self-possession—the might which is the sole right not to be a slave! Do you see?

DEBORAH
I see, Dear—that you have gone very far away from me—and become lost in yourself and very lonely.

SIMON
Lost? Oh no, don't imagine I have lost. I always win. Wait and see, Mother! I'll prove to you I can lead the Company to a glorious, final triumph—complete independence and freedom within itself!

He pauses and looks around the garden. Then he sighs wearily.

But sometimes lately, Mother, alone in my office, I have felt so weary of the game—of watching suspiciously each card I led to myself from across the table—even though I had marked them all—watching my winnings pile up and becoming confused with losses—feeling my swindler's victorious gloating die into boredom and discontent—the flame of ambition smoulder into a chill dismay—as though that opponent within had spat an extinguishing poison of disdain—

DEBORAH
Strangely, tenderly sympathetic.
I used to know so well.
Tensely.
I had once reached a point where I had grown so lost, I had not even a dream left I could dream without screaming scornful laughter at myself. I would sit locked in the summer-house here—sit there for hours in wisdom-ridiculing contemplation of myself, and spit in my mind, and my heart, like a village idiot in a country store spitting at the belly of a stove—cursing the day I was born, the day I indifferently conceived, the day I bore—
With a terrible intensity.
Until I swear to you I felt I could by just one tiny further wish, one little effort more of will, push open the door to madness where I could at least believe in a dream again! And how I longed for that final escape!
She suddenly turns and stares at him with hatred.
Ah! And you wonder why I hate you!
Abruptly overcome by a panic of dread, starting to her feet.
Simon! What are you trying to do? Leave me alone! Leave the past in its forgotten grave!
Trying to control herself and be casual and indifferent.
Frankly, I am bored with listening to your nonsense. I will go in the house now. Sara must be wondering what is keeping me, now the sun is setting.
She starts for the path off left. Simon, without looking

at her, begins to speak again. She stops, makes herself go on, finally stops and turns to stare at him.

SIMON

I began to remember lately—and long for this garden—and you, as you used to be and are no longer—and I as I was then—in this safe haven, where we could repose our souls in fantasy—evade, escape, forget, rest in peace! I regret that paradise in which you were the good, kind, beloved, beautiful Queen. I have become so weary of what they call life beyond the wall, Mother.

DEBORAH

Moved and fascinated, takes a step toward him—tenderly.

I see you have, my son. Who knows?—your loss is not irrevocable. We—you and I—in partnership in a new company of the pure spirit, might reorganize your bankruptcy—if I may put it in terms you understand.

She smiles teasingly.

SIMON

With a passionate eagerness.

Yes!

He grabs her hand.

DEBORAH

As if the touch of his hand alarmed her—shrinks back, turning away from him—guiltily stammers to herself.

No! I swore to her I would never interfere. I cannot! I am content. I have all I desire.

She turns to Simon—resentfully and derisively.

My dear boy, your childish fancies are ridiculous. We do not really wish such nonsense. And if we did, it would be impossible, we have both changed so much.

Carelessly taunting.

But if you care to drop in here once in a while on your return from work, I know the children would be pleased to see you. You could boast to them of your heroic exploits.

SIMON

Stiffens, stares at her with hatred for a second—then coldly, in a curt tone.

I'm glad you mentioned the children. It reminds me of my real purpose in coming here. I must inform you that Sara and I have decided you are having a very bad influence on our children—

DEBORAH

Startled—resentful and uneasy.

That is ridiculous! I have been at pains not to influence them at all!

SIMON

Sara decided that henceforth the children must be forbidden to see you except in the house when either she or I are present to protect them.

DEBORAH

Strickenly.

You mean they are to be taken from me? I am to be left entirely alone again—with no life but the memory of the past—? You can't be so cruel! I have made myself love them! I have created a new life—

Abruptly—with an eager hatred.

And you say Sara decided this? No! I won't believe it!

SIMON

I would hardly lie about something you can confirm as soon as you see her. You'll find she is giving them their orders in the house right now.

DEBORAH

With an almost joyous vindictiveness.

Ah, if she has betrayed me and broken all her pledges! That releases me!

SIMON

You know there is nothing strange about her being jealous of your stealing her children.

DEBORAH

With a vindictive satisfaction.

Well, perhaps she has cause to be! They can never forget me! You are right! I have never entirely trusted her! I have resented her interference and possessiveness—I have hated the intolerable debt of daily gratitude!

Then brokenly.

But how could she do this to me! She knows how much the children have meant to me! She knows without them I shall be lost again!

SIMON

Come now, Mother. You are not really as exercised by the loss of the children as you pretend. You were never intended for the job of Sara's unpaid nursemaid. I have seen you fall completely under Sara's influence and become merely a female, common, vulgar—a greedy home-owner, dreamless and contented!

DEBORAH

Angrily.

You are talking nonsense! It is I who have influenced her! Deliberately! As part of my scheme!

Hastily.

No! What made me say that?

SIMON

With a resentful intensity.

By God, there have been times when, as I watched you together in the house at night, she would seem to steal all identity from you—until there was but one woman—she!

DEBORAH

With an exultant satisfaction.

Ah, you felt that? That we were one, united against—? That is what I wished to do! Poor boy! But you are blind or you would have seen it was I who took possession of her in order to—

She checks herself.

But as you say, it is very confusing. One cannot see clearly what or why—

Frightenedly.

And I do not care to see. Besides, you have shown me clearly I do not need her to take back what is mine.

SIMON

Staring before him.

Yes, Mother, I rely on you to help me keep her in her rightful place hereafter.

DEBORAH

Regards him calculatingly—then with a caressingly gentle air.

And my place?

SIMON

With queer, hesitating embarrassment.

Why, here in your garden, of course, as always in the past.

DEBORAH

Softly insinuating.

Alone? I was not always alone in the past.

She pats his hair—with a teasing laugh.

What? Have you no hope to offer your poor lonely mother?

SIMON

Awkwardly stiff and formal.

I do not wish you to be too lonely. I will be happy to consider any suggestion you—

DEBORAH

With a teasing laugh, ruffling his hair playfully.

Ah! I see! Still Napoleon! Still so proud! Very well. I will play your humble slave, Sire. Will you deign to visit me here and comfort my exile?

SIMON

Stiffly.

Yes, it is very restful here.

Eagerly, under his awkward formality.

I shall be delighted to drop in and keep you company here for a while each afternoon on my way home. A little rest here each day will restore the soul—the change I so badly need—

He breaks off. He sees the volume of Byron on the steps.

He picks it up—with a forced casual air.

What's this? Ah, Byron—

He examines the volume—with pleased boyish surprise.
I thought this looked familiar. Here's the inscription "To my beloved mother." Here are the parts I marked, and the parts you marked, and the parts we marked together. Do you remember, Mother, we would be sitting here just as we are now, and I'd ask you to read aloud to me—?

DEBORAH
Softly.
I remember, Dear, as clearly as if it were yesterday. Or, even, as though it were now.

SIMON
Turns the pages.
Here is our favorite! I don't have to look at the book. I still know it by heart. But I'll bet you can guess what it is, Mother.

DEBORAH
Smiling fondly.
Yes, I'm sure I can guess—
She recites—with growing arrogance.
"I have not loved the World, nor the World me;
I have not flattered its rank breath,—"

SIMON
Breaks in and takes it up, taking on her tone.
"—nor bowed
To its idolatries a patient knee,
Nor coined my cheek to smiles,—"

DEBORAH
"—nor cried aloud
In worship of an echo:"

SIMON
His face hardening into his office mask of the ruthless executive.
"—in the crowd
They could not deem me one of such—"

DEBORAH
"—I stood

Among them, but not of them—"
He joins in here and they both finish together.
"—in a shroud
Of thoughts which were not their thoughts,—"
They stop abruptly and stare at each other—then they both burst out laughing merrily, and Deborah claps her hands.

SIMON

I remember so well now, Mother!

DEBORAH

Yes, that was just as it used to be.
From the house off left Sara's voice is heard calling in a tone of repressed uneasiness: "Simon, are you in the garden?" The two start resentfully. Deborah gives him a hostile, contemptuous look.
She wants her husband.

SIMON

Angrily, as if aloud to himself.
God, can I never know a moment's freedom!
He calls curtly, almost insultingly.
I am here with Mother. What do you want now?
Sara's voice answers with an attempt at carelessness: "Nothing, Darling. I simply wanted to be sure." A door is heard closing.

SIMON

With a gloating chuckle.
She wants to be sure. I thought she sounded a little uneasy.

DEBORAH

With a malicious smile.
Even a little frightened perhaps.

SIMON

Frowning.
I have already ordered her never to come here again.
Eagerly insistent.

Let's forget her existence. We were back in the past before she lived in us.

DEBORAH

Take my hand so you will not get lost.

SIMON

Kisses her hand with a shy, boyish impulsiveness.

I will never leave you again, Mother. Do you know what had come into my mind? A memory that goes back long before our Byron days, when I was still at the fairy-tale age, and you would read tales aloud to me, here. Or, what I liked better, you would make up your own. They seemed so much more real than the book ones.

DEBORAH

Uneasily, forcing a laugh.

Good Heavens, you are going far back! I had forgotten—

SIMON

Insistently, almost commandingly.

You can't have forgotten the one I just remembered. It was your favorite. And mine. I can see you sitting there, as you are now, dressed all in white, so beautiful and so unreal, more like a character in your story than a flesh-and-blood mother. One would have thought you were afraid that even your own child was a greedy interloper plotting to steal you from your dreams!

DEBORAH

Uneasily and guiltily—forcing a laugh.

Why, what a mean suspicious thought—about your poor devoted mother, Dear!

SIMON

You would be sitting there before the summer-house, like a sentry guarding the door.

He turns to her resentfully.

Why did you make that silly rule that no one was ever allowed to go in the summer-house but you? As if it were some secret temple of which you were high priestess! No one would have cared about going in there, anyway!

DEBORAH

You used to plead and beg—

SIMON

Well, naturally, when you forbid a boy to go anywhere, without giving him any sensible reason—

DEBORAH

A bit sharply, as if he were still the little boy.

I explained over and over again that I felt all the rooms in the house, even my bedroom, were your father's property. And this garden I shared with you. I naturally desired one place, no matter how tiny, that would be mine alone. It's just that you stubbornly refused to believe that. You didn't want to admit I could live, even for a moment, without you.

With a shiver—hurriedly.

Why do you remember that so well? You were starting to remember a fairy tale.

SIMON

There is a connection with the summer-house.

DEBORAH

Startled.

Then I do not care to hear—

SIMON

Oh, not in your story. The connection was in my imagination.

He begins to tell the story, staring before him as if he visualized it.

There was once upon a time a young King of a happy land who, through the evil magic of a beautiful enchantress, had been dispossessed of his realm and banished to wander over the world, a homeless, unhappy outcast. Now the enchantress, it appeared, had in a last moment of remorse, when he was being sent into exile, revealed to him that there was a way in which he might regain his lost kingdom. He must search the world for a certain magic door.

DEBORAH

Ah.

SIMON

It might be any door, but if he wished to find it with all his heart, he would recognize it when he came to it, and know that on the other side was his lost kingdom. After enduring bitter trials, and numberless disappointments, he at last found himself before a door, and the wish in his heart told him his quest was ended. But just as he was about to open it and cross the threshold, he heard the voice of the enchantress speaking from the other side, for she was there awaiting his coming. "Wait. Before you open I must warn you to remember how evil I can be and that it is probable I maliciously lied and gave you a false hope. If you dare to open the door you may discover this is no longer your old happy realm but a barren desert, where it is always night, haunted by terrible ghosts and ruled over by a hideous old witch, who wishes to destroy your claim to her realm, and the moment you cross the threshold she will tear you to pieces and devour you."

DEBORAH
With a little shudder—forcing a laugh.
Oh, come now, Dear. I am sure I never— I remember the story as an ironically humorous tale.

SIMON
"So you had better be sure of your courage," the enchantress called warningly, "and remember that as long as you stay where you are you will run no risk of anything worse than your present unhappy exile." Then he heard her laugh. She did not speak again, although he knew she remained there, and would always remain, waiting to see if he would dare open the door.
With a strange bitterness.
But he never did, you said. He felt she was lying to test his courage. Yet, at the same time, he felt she was not lying, and he was afraid. He wanted to turn his back on the door and go far away, but it held him in a spell and he could never leave it. So he remained for the rest of his life standing before the door, and became a beggar, whining for alms from all who passed by.
He turns to stare at her—forcing a smile, resentfully.
That, I suppose, constitutes the humorous irony you remembered?

DEBORAH

Laughingly, with an undercurrent of taunting satisfaction.
Yes, I can remember how resentful you were at the ending. You used to insist I imagine a new ending in which the wicked enchantress had become a good fairy and opened the door and welcomed him home and they were both happy ever after.
She laughs.

SIMON

And you would laugh at me.
With a strange challenging look.
I would still like to discover if you could possibly imagine a happy ending to that tale.

DEBORAH

What silly nonsense, Simon! Fairy tales, indeed! What a preoccupation for a Napoleon of facts!

SIMON

Yes, absurd, I admit. But I was very impressionable then and your story was very real to me. The door of the tale became identified in my mind with the door there to your forbidden summer-house. I used to boast to myself that if I were that King I would gamble recklessly on the chance—
Suddenly, moved by a strange urgency, he springs to his feet and goes past her up the steps to the door.
Let's have done with this mystery right now!
He seizes the knob.

DEBORAH

Starts to her feet in a panic of dread and grabs his other arm.
No, Simon! No!
Her panic is transformed into an outraged fury.
Come away! Obey me this instant! How dare you! Will your vulgar greed leave me nothing I can call my own?

SIMON

Overcome by this outburst, moves back down the steps obediently like a cowed boy.
I'm sorry, Mother. I— I didn't think you'd mind now—

DEBORAH

Suddenly calm and relieved and a bit guilty.

I can't help minding. The truth is I have become superstitious—remembering the last time I was in there—and I was afraid—

SIMON

Has recovered his poise as she has weakened—curtly.

That is damned nonsense, Mother. There's nothing there, of course.

DEBORAH

With a little shiver.

I am there.

SIMON

That's insanity, Mother.

DEBORAH

Yes. I know. There is nothing in there but dark and dust and spiderwebs—and the silence of dead dreams.

SIMON

Smiling.

Well, anyway, it would not be a happy ending, would it, for me to go in alone? No, someday, I will give you the courage to open the door yourself and we will go together—

DEBORAH

Turning on him with forced scorn.

It is grotesque for a grown man to act so childishly. I forbid you ever to mention this subject again. It is only on that condition I can agree to welcome you in my garden.

SIMON

With a mocking gallantry, kissing her hand.

Your wish my law, Madame.

DEBORAH

Abruptly changing to a gay, arrogantly-pleased, seductive coquetry.

That is as should be, Monsieur.

From the house off left comes Sara's voice: "Simon, are you still in the garden?"

SIMON

Exasperatedly.

Yes! What do you want of me now?

A pause. Then Sara's voice comes, hurt and a little forlorn: "Nothing, Darling. It's getting near supper time, that's all." *Her voice suddenly takes on a resentful commanding tone:* "It's time you came in, do you hear me?"

DEBORAH

With a bitter, jealous derisiveness.

Your slut commands you now!

She calls, with an undertone of gloating mockery.

Don't worry, Sara. I'll bring him back to you.

She gets up. He also rises. She speaks with a cruel eagerness.

Let us go in—together. I am eager to see her. I want to see how frightened she is.

She takes his arm—tenderly.

Oh, I am so happy—so very happy, Dear!—to have my son again!

SIMON

Not half so happy as I am to have my mother again!

They start to go off, left. Abruptly he stops—in a tone of warning advice made more effective by a provocative hint of taunting behind it.

But remember she is strong, too. Take care that the moment you see her you do not surrender to her influence again. I know you do not want her laughing at you up her sleeve any more, as she has been doing.

DEBORAH

With growing anger—blurts out.

Laughing at me! The stupid vulgar fool! If she only knew! It is I who have been laughing in my mind at her! It is singular that such a conquering Napoleon cannot recognize a complete victory and a crushing defeat when he sees them!

SIMON

Stares at her with a curious, objectively appraising look—then with a satisfied nod.

Yes, make yourself believe that, Mother, and you can safely defy her. After all, there is a great deal of truth in that aspect of it, as I have suspected. Your truth, of course—not Sara's—nor mine. And not even the whole of your truth. But you and I can wait to discover what that is later on.

He smiles with pleasant casualness.

Just now I think we had better go in to supper.

DEBORAH
Pulling away, stares at him with a puzzled frightened dread.

Simon! What—?

Conquering her fear and suddenly gloating, takes his arm—eagerly.

Yes! Let us go in. I can't wait to tell her you are going to be with me each evening, that you are now my own dear son again!

SIMON
Sharply commanding.

No! Not until I give you permission to speak. You will kindly not forget, Mother, all this reorganization of my home is my affair and must be carried out exactly as I have calculated. You had better not interfere if you expect me ever to keep you company. Come. It is getting late.

She is again looking at him with bewildered dread, has shrunk back, taking her hand from his arm. But he ignores this and grasps her arm and makes her walk off beside him up the path to the house.

CURTAIN

Act Two, Scene Three

Scene   Parlor of the Harford mansion—a high-ceilinged, finely-
proportioned room such as one finds in the Massachusetts
houses designed by Bulfinch or McIntire and built in the
late 1790s. The walls and ceiling are white. A rug covers
most of the floor of waxed dark wood. A crystal chandelier
hangs from the middle of the ceiling at center. At extreme
left-front a small table against the wall, then a door leading to the entrance hall, another chair, and, farther back,
a table. In the middle of the rear wall is the door to
Simon's study. On either side of it, a chair facing front.
Against the right wall, toward rear, another table.
Farther forward, a high window looking out on the street,
then a chair, and finally at right-front, a fireplace. At
left-rear of the fireplace is a long sofa with a small table
and reading-lamp by its left end. Toward front, at left,
is an oval table with another lamp. A chair is by right-
rear of this table, facing right-front. Another chair is at
left-front of this table, facing directly front. It is around
nine o'clock at night of the same day.

As the curtain rises, Sara is sitting in the chair at left-
front of the table, Simon across the table from her in the
chair at rear-right of it, and Deborah on the left end of
the sofa by the lamp. Sara is pretending to work on a
piece of needle-point. Deborah has a book in her hands,
but she stares over it. Simon also holds a book and keeps
his eyes fixed on it, but his eyes do not move. The two
women wear semi-formal evening gowns, Deborah's all
white, Sara's a blue that matches the color of her eyes.
Simon is dressed in black.

For a moment after the curtain rises there is an atmosphere
of tense quiet in the room, an eavesdropping silence that
waits, holding its breath and straining its ears. Then, as

though the meaning of the silence were becoming audible, their thoughts are heard.

SARA

Thinking.

You'd think taking the children away meant nothing to her—No, I know she loved them—it's her great-lady pride won't give me the satisfaction to know she's hurt— And there's something more behind it—I thought they'd never come in—I heard them laughing—and when they came she looked as gay as you please—something about him, too—sly—like there was a secret between them—

DEBORAH

Thinking.

In the garden, at the end, I was so sure of him—but—he changed when he saw her— She was not half as frightened as I hoped—When he tells her he is coming to my garden every evening—that he is my son again— Why does he wait?

SARA

Reassuring herself—thinking.

Ah, I'm a fool to waste a thought on her— Even the part of him that belongs to the Company will be mine now—all of him—and my children, too, will be all mine!— This is my home!— Let her keep to her garden—let her sit and dream herself into a madhouse!

DEBORAH

Thinking.

She is only pretending to work on her needle-point— Yes, quite as frightened as Simon and I had hoped— She will become no more than the empty name of wife, a housekeeper, a mother of children, our Irish biddy nurse girl and house servant!

SIMON

Thinking.

They do not sit together on the sofa as has been their wont—I am where I belong between them—two women—opposites—whose lives have meaning only in so far as they live within my living—Henceforth this is my home and I own my own mind again!

He smiles to himself gloatingly and begins to read. As if their minds had partly sensed the tenor of his thought, the two women turn to stare at him, with a stirring of suspicion and resentment. They both look quickly away.

SARA
Thinking.

He isn't reading—just pretending to—smiling to himself—sly—

DEBORAH
Thinking.

What is he thinking, I wonder? —of the Company and this secretary-mistress he boasted of— I hate that smug, lustful, greedy trader's smile of his!

SARA
Thinking.

I know that smile—when he's managed a foxy deal for the Company— I hope he doesn't think he'll cheat me— I was a fool to let him see I wanted him so much!—

DEBORAH
Thinking.

This is stupid! —to make myself uneasy—after he's proved so conclusively— I'll be sensible now and read my book—

She begins to read determinedly. There is a pause in which each of the three attends to the matter in hand. It is Simon who stops first. His eyes cease reading and stare at the book preoccupiedly.

SIMON
Thinking—frowning.

I control the game now and can have it played as I wish— But it means I must always remain in the game myself—be as careful and watchful now outside the office as in it—never relax my vigilance— There is always the danger of alliance of conniving enemies—an unceasing duel to the death with life!

SARA
Has stopped sewing—thinking.

I feel something is staring over my shoulder— It's strange here tonight— It's not the home it's been—not like home at all—no peace—

Unconsciously she sighs regretfully.

She and I would be sitting together on the sofa, laughing and telling each other about the children—he sitting alone, thinking out schemes for his Company—not bothering us—

DEBORAH

Has stopped reading—thinking.

How tense the quiet is in this house tonight—as though a bomb were concealed in the room with a fuse slowly sputtering toward— And the silence waits—hands clapped over its ears—

Unconsciously she sighs regretfully.

So changed from what it was last night— We would laugh together, thinking of the children—I had forgotten him sitting alone there—

SIMON

Thinking—uneasily.

Perhaps I should have waited— What made their petty sentimental women's world assume such a false importance for me?

SARA

Thinking—regretfully.

He's a fool to think she could ever have taken my children—I can keep what's mine—

DEBORAH

Thinking—regretfully.

I have grown to lean upon her health and strength—as one leans against a tree, deep-rooted in the common earth—

SIMON

Thinking.

What the devil possessed me to ask Sara to come to the office? Now I won't have a separate man's life free of woman even there!

He turns to stare at her with a vindictive hostility.

SARA

Thinking.

Treating his wife as if she was a whore he'd pick up on the street and ask her price!—

> *She turns to stare at him with a revengeful hostility. As they meet each other's eyes, each turns away guiltily. Forcing a casual tone, she speaks to him.*

Yes, Simon? You were going to say something?

SIMON
In a like casual tone.
I? No. I thought you—

SARA
No.

SIMON
I was preoccupied with my thoughts.

SARA
So was I.

SIMON
I was thinking of Mother, as it happens.

SARA
That's strange. So was I.
> *Neither of them looks at Deborah. A pause.*

DEBORAH
Thinking—resentfully.
He lied—he said that to hurt her— Much as I ought to hate her, I pity her when I see him deliberately trying to humiliate—

SIMON
Thinking—resentfully.
By that lie I've put Mother back in my mind— Good God, I'll be playing with toys next, and begging her to tell me a fairy tale!
> *He stares at her with vindictive hostility.*

DEBORAH
Thinking.
His proposal to visit me each evening—as if he were doing me a

favor—I never even wanted him to be conceived—I was glad to be rid of him when he was born— He had made my beauty grotesquely ugly by his presence, bloated and misshapen— And then the compulsion to love him after he was born—
> *She turns to stare at him with vindictive hostility. Then, as each meets the other's eyes, each turns away guiltily.*

SIMON
Speaks—forcing a casual tone.
Yes, Mother? You wanted to say something?

DEBORAH
Echoing his tone.
No. I thought you—

SIMON
No. I was thinking of Sara.

DEBORAH
That is strange, I was thinking of her, too.
> *Neither of them looks at Sara. A pause.*

SARA
Thinking—resentfully.
Poor woman! She can't read—she's thinking how she'll miss the children—alone all day— He'll have me at the office— Alone in the past— He'll have her in an asylum in the end!— It's a terrible thing he can hate his own mother so!—

DEBORAH
Thinking.
She had begun to look upon me as a second mother—and I was happy to regard her as my daughter—because her strength and health and acceptance of life gave me a faith in my own living— and now he dares to take that security away from me!—to offer me in exchange ghosts from the past to haunt me—

SARA
Thinking.
I'm not a thought he moves around in his mind to suit his pleasure—

DEBORAH
Thinking.

If she'd sit with me here as on other nights, we'd understand and forgive each other—

> *They both speak to each other simultaneously: "Sara" "Deborah." They bend forward so they can see each other past him and smile at each other with a relieved understanding. Deborah speaks with a strange gentleness.*

Yes, Daughter. I ought to have known you guessed my thoughts.

SARA
Getting up—with a quiet smile.

I hope you guessed mine. May I come and sit with you?

DEBORAH

I was going to ask you to.

> *Sara goes around the table and passes behind Simon, ignoring him, and goes to the sofa. Deborah pats the sofa on her left, smiling an affectionate welcome.*

This is your place, beside me.

SARA
Bends impulsively and gives her a daughterly kiss on the cheek.

I know.

> *She sits down, close beside her, so their arms touch.*

SIMON
Thinking—with contemptuous relief.

Ah, so they have decided to forget and forgive— This hate was becoming a living presence in the room—and in my mind— But now we will be back where we were on other nights. Meanwhile, keeping an eye on them to make sure this sentimental reunion is not too successful— But each is lying and acting, of course— playing the hypocrite in the hope of gaining some advantage— It will be amusing to watch.

SARA
Turns to Deborah with impulsive frankness.

I want to beg your forgiveness, Mother—about the children. It was mean of me not to trust you.

123

DEBORAH

Takes her hand—gently.

One cannot help being jealous. It is part of the curse of love.

SARA

With a quick resentful look at Simon.

Yes, you do feel cursed by it when it's too greedy.

DEBORAH

Patting Sara's hand.

Thank goodness, we've understood each other and what might have developed into a stupid quarrel is all forgotten now, isn't it?

Presses her hand and keeps it in hers.

I had begun to feel so weak and at the mercy of the past.

SARA

Shame on you. And you with four handsome grandchildren to love, and everything in life to live for.

DEBORAH

Then I may have the children back?

SARA

Indeed you may! And remember I wasn't really the one who took them away from you.

She casts a resentful look at Simon.

DEBORAH

You are so kind and generous. I hate myself for having permitted my mind to be tempted—

She gives Simon a bitter hostile look—then quickly to Sara.

But that's over.

A pause. The two women sit with clasped hands, their faces relieved, affectionate and contented, staring defiantly at Simon.

SARA

I know how unhappy you felt. I was miserable myself over there, with him between us.

DEBORAH

Glancing at Simon resentfully—lowering her voice to a whisper.

Yes. That's just it, Sara. We must never again allow him to come between—

They bend closer to each other until their heads are about touching, and all during the following scene talk in whispers, their eyes fixed on Simon.

SARA

Men are never content.

DEBORAH

Beginning to smile.

He was always a greedy, jealous boy. That's where we may have him at our mercy. His jealousy drives him to need us. But we already have four sons—

SARA

Beginning to smile, too.

And so we don't have to need him.

She laughs softly and jeeringly. Simon stirs uneasily and his eyes cease to follow the lines. He stares at the page.

DEBORAH

Laughs with Sara.

It is really he who is helpless and lost—and completely at our mercy!

SIMON

Thinking—with a tense dread.

I still feel hatred like a living presence in this room—strange—drawing close—surrounding—threatening—*me*— But that's absurd—they hate each other now—

Frightenedly.

But it has become dark in here and Mother and Sara have vanished— Mother took her hand and led her back—as if she opened a door into the past in whose darkness they vanished to reappear as one woman—a woman recalling Mother but a strange woman—unreal, a ghost inhumanly removed from living, beautiful and coldly remote and proud—with a smile deliberately amused by its own indifference—because she no longer wants me—has taken all she needed— I have served my purpose—she has ruthlessly got rid of me—she is free—and I am left lost in myself, with nothing!

He has dropped the book in his lap and straightened himself tensely, gripping the arms of his chair, staring before him frightenedly. As his thoughts have progressed the expressions on the two women's faces have mirrored his description as though, subconsciously, their mood was created by his mind. They become proudly arrogant and coldly indifferent to him. He goes on thinking with increasing dread.

But her nature has changed—she stares at me with hate—she is revengeful and evil—a cannibal witch whose greed will devour!

Their expressions have changed to revengeful, gloating cruelty and they stare at him with hate. He starts forward in his chair as if he were about to fly in horror from the room.

DEBORAH
Smiling gloatingly.
See, Sara, he is not even pretending to read now.

SARA
Smiling gloatingly.
As scared as if he saw a ghost!

DEBORAH
Her expression softens to a condescending maternal tenderness.
Perhaps we are being too hard on him. What he has tried to do has been so obviously childish and futile.

SARA
It's because he's jealous, and that proves how much he loves us.

DEBORAH
Yes, I think we should merely be amused, as we would be at the mischief of a bad sulky boy.

SARA
Smilingly—complacently maternal.

And forgive him if he promises not to do it again.

DEBORAH
Speaks to Simon with an amused, teasing smile.
Wake up, Dear.
He starts and turns to stare at them bewilderedly.
Why do you stare like that?

SARA
You might be more polite to your ladies, Darling.

SIMON
As if suddenly emerging from a spell—with an impulsive grateful relief.
I beg your pardon. I must have dozed off and dreamed—

DEBORAH
My poor boy! Do tell us what you dreamed.
He ignores her. She laughs teasingly.
He won't do it, Sara. But we know he is very uneasy now, not sure of himself at all, wondering what we will decide to do about him.

SARA
With a little laugh.
Yes, he has a guilty conscience and he knows he ought to be punished.

SIMON
As if he hadn't heard them, but confusedly apologetic and apprehensive, avoiding their eyes.
I—I am afraid I interrupted a private discussion. Pray continue. I am interested in this book—

DEBORAH
Smiles at him now, cajolingly affectionate.
We have agreed to forgive you, Dear—just because you are such a silly jealous boy.

SARA
Come over here and sit with us now. You look so lost over there alone.

> *She moves over and pats the sofa between her and Deborah—enticingly.*

Look, you can sit here and have love all around you. You'll be between us, as you've been trying to be.

DEBORAH

> *She pats the sofa invitingly.*

Come, Dear.

> *He does not seem to hear.*

Still so vain and stubborn?

> *To Sara.*

Well, since the mountain is too proud to come to Mahomet—

> *She takes Sara's hand and they rise. Their arms around each other's waists, they advance on Simon with mocking, enticing smiles. They are like two mothers who, confident of their charm, take a possessive gratification in teasing a young, bashful son. But there is something more behind this—the calculating coquetry of two prostitutes trying to entice a man.*

We must humor his manly pride, Sara. Anything to keep peace in our home!

> *She laughs.*

SARA

> *Laughingly.*

Yes. Anything to give him his way, as long as it's our way!

> *They have come to Simon who stares as if he did not notice their approach, and yet instinctively shrinks back in his chair. They group together in back of him, Deborah at left-rear and Sara at right-rear of his chair. They bend over, each with an arm about the other, until their faces touch the side of his head. Their other arms go around him so that their hands touch on his chest.*

DEBORAH

Why are you so afraid of us?

SARA

We're not going to eat you, Darling, if you are that sweet.
Their arms hug him.

SIMON

*Thinking—with a mingling of fascinated dread and an
anguished yearning.*

I cannot keep them separate—they are too strong here in their
home—they unite against the invader— But I must remember
they only seem to become one— But I feel her arms around me—
and she is good now, not evil—she loves me—and so I can surrender and be hers—

*He relaxes with a dreamy smile of content in their arms
and murmurs drowsily in gentle wonder.*

And I have won the deciding victory over them!

*He gives a strange chuckle of satisfaction, and closes
his eyes.*

DEBORAH

You see, Sara. There was no cause for us to be afraid. I can always,
whenever I wish, make him my little boy again.

She kisses him on the cheek.

Can't I, Dear?

SARA

Gives her a quick resentful jealous look.

I wasn't the one who was afraid. Don't I know whenever I want,
I can make him my lover again, who'd give anything he has for
me!

She kisses his other cheek.

Can't I, Darling?

*She and Deborah suddenly turn and stare at each other
with defiant, jealous enmity over his head, pulling their
hands away so they no longer touch on his chest, but each
still holding him. Simon starts and stiffens in his chair.*

SIMON

No!

*Jerks forward to his feet from their arms. They each give
a frightened pleading cry. He turns to stare from one to*

the other for a moment in a dazed awakening confusion, stammering.

Ah! You are both there. I thought— I beg your pardon— I must have dozed off again—

Then curtly and rudely.

Well, now that the little farce is over, if you will permit me to sit, and return where you belong—

The two women's faces grow cold and hostile and defiant. But they are also full of dread.

DEBORAH
Takes Sara's hand.

Come, Sara.

They pass behind him to sit on the sofa, side by side as before, clasping each other's hand. They stare at Simon defiantly and apprehensively. He sits in his chair and stares at his book again.

SIMON
Suddenly looks up, but avoids their eyes.

For God's sake, why do you stare like that?

He snaps his book shut and springs to his feet—angrily, to conceal his apprehension.

Can I never have a moment's privacy in my own home? I work like a slave all day to stuff your insatiable maws with luxury and security for the rearing of children! Is it too much to ask in return that I be permitted a little peace of mind at night here? I will not tolerate any more of your interference! If you persist in it, I will be compelled to force either one or the other of you to leave my home—and my life!—forever! That is my final warning!

He turns toward the door at left, avoiding their eyes.

I'm going to my study. Hereafter, I shall spend my evenings there alone, and you may do as you please. Tear this house apart, devour each other, if you must, until only one of you survives! After all, that would be one solution— But leave me alone!

He strides to the study door and opens it—then turns and murmurs.

I— I beg your pardon for being rude— I am worn out—have

worked too hard on this railroad deal—and now I have it, I seem
to have nothing—

> *He pauses. Suddenly he has the beaten quality of one
> begging for pity. But they remain staring as one at him,
> their eyes hard and unforgiving.*

You—you know how much I love each of you—it is only when
you unite to dispossess me that you compel me to defend my
right to what is mine—all I ask is that each of you keep your
proper place in my mind—

> *Abruptly his tone becomes slyly taunting.*

But I am forgetting I arranged all that today. I will leave you now
to inform each other of the secret you are each so cunningly
concealing.

> *He smiles sneeringly, but is afraid to meet their eyes. He
> turns quickly, goes into his study, and locks the door.
> They stare at the door. There is a moment's silence.*

DEBORAH

> *Slowly, hardly above a whisper, but with a taunting,
> threatening scorn in her tone.*

I have a suspicion, Sara, that our big jealous boy has become very
frightened and wishes now he hadn't been so wicked—now, when
it's too late.

SARA

I have the same suspicion myself, Deborah.

DEBORAH

> *Hesitates uneasily—then trying desperately to be confi-
> dently matter-of-fact, and forcing a smile.*

Then I think we can now safely tell each other what the arrangements he spoke of are. As far as I am concerned, I was hiding mine
from you only because he said he wished to tell you and made me
promise I wouldn't.

SARA

He did the same with me.

> *With a sudden underlying hostility.*

I was only too eager to let you know.

> *Guiltily.*

I mean—

131

DEBORAH
Stiffening.

I think not any more eager than I was—
She checks herself. Then says gently.

Tell me your secret, Daughter. Whatever it is, I will remember it is his doing, and I will understand.

SARA

Thank you, Mother. And I'll understand when you tell me—
She blurts out hastily with an undercurrent of guilty defiance.

He got me to agree to work with him at his office from now on. I'm to start tomorrow—

DEBORAH
Startled and unable to conceal an uprush of jealous hate.

Ah! Then you are the woman he boasted he was living with as a—
Instinctively she withdraws her hand from Sara's.

SARA
Bitterly.

You said you'd understand!

DEBORAH
Contritely—grabbing her hand again.

I will! I do!

SARA

I'm to be his secretary and a secret partner. He seemed so nervous and tired out and distracted, and he asked me wouldn't I please help him with his work and share— You can understand that, Deborah?

DEBORAH
Sneeringly.

I can. I know only too well how greedy—
Fighting this back—guiltily.

I mean, it is your right.

SARA
Defensively.

It's my right, surely. I'm glad you admit that. He said he was so lonely. He said he missed me so much and wouldn't I let him have a life just with me again. He said I was still so beautiful to him and I knew he was telling the truth.

DEBORAH

Ah!

She again jerks her hand away.

SARA

I'm sorry. I didn't mean to boast.
She reaches for Deborah's hand again.
But wait till you hear the rest. I could feel the change in him as he is now in his office—that he's grown so greedy and unscrupulous and used to having his own way that if I refused him, he'd only buy another woman. You can understand that, can't you? You're a woman, too.

DEBORAH
Tensely.
I am making myself understand. Besides, this has nothing to do with me. It is entirely your business.

SARA

Yes, business. If you think I liked him insulting his wife and acting as if I was a street whore—

DEBORAH

Why should I think of it, Sara? But—you appealed to me as a woman, didn't you? You mean forget he is anything to me? I can. I have forgotten him several times before in my life—completely, as if he had never been born. That is what he has never forgiven. If I were in your place I would hate him, and I would revenge myself by becoming what he wished me to be! I would make him pay for me until I had taken everything he possessed! And when he had no more to pay me, I would drive him out of my life to beg outside my door!

SARA
With a vindictive smile—strangely.
I felt exactly like that!

Abruptly changing the subject.
But now tell me what he made you agree to.

DEBORAH

He begged me to give him a life alone with me again away from his office and his home.

SARA

Stares at her suspiciously.
What do you mean?
Instinctively she starts to pull her hand away.

DEBORAH

You promised to understand. He begged me to let him keep me company in my garden every evening from now on. And, as I knew how lonely I would be in the future without the children—

SARA

But I've told you you'll have them back.

DEBORAH

No, Sara, you are very generous, but I really will not need them, now that I have my own son again.

SARA

Gives way to a flash of jealous, uneasy anger.
Ah, and so that's what it is! I've always known if you were ever given the chance—!
She jerks her hand from Deborah's.

DEBORAH

Pleading now frightenedly, grabbing Sara's hand.
Sara! You promised to remember! The truth is—I didn't want him in my garden ever again. He made himself appear like a little boy again, so forlorn and lost in himself—needing my love so terribly! So I couldn't help but consent. As a mother, you can understand that, Sara!

SARA

You've a right. And I'll have my own sons all to myself now. I'll have him all day at the office. No, you're entirely welcome. And when I think of all he's done today to make us hate each other—I tell you, as woman to woman, I'd let him go back and back into the past until he got so lost in his dreams he'd be no more a man at all, but a timid little boy hiding from life behind my skirts!

DEBORAH

I do not think we have anything to fear, Sara. In a very short time he will beg us on his knees to restore that peace and take him back into our home again.

SARA

And won't I laugh to see him beg!

DEBORAH

We will both laugh.

They laugh softly together.

But we must trust each other and never let him make us hate each other! Let us swear that again, Sara!

SARA

I swear I won't!

DEBORAH

And I swear!

She smiles contentedly and pats Sara's hand.

That's settled, then. Now I think we can be as we have been.

SARA

Yes, and it's a help to have him out of the room.

With a change of tone to that of the doting mother.

Tell me about the children when they were with you, like you always do.

DEBORAH

Of course I will.

She pauses—trying to remember.

I can't seem to— I'm afraid I have entirely forgotten, Sara.

SARA

Piqued—resentfully.

You've always remembered before.

DEBORAH

Reproachfully.

Now! I know I have, but— A lot of things have happened since then to disturb my mind.

SARA

Ah, don't I know.

Uneasily.

And they're still happening—even if he is locked in his study. I can still feel his thoughts reaching out—

DEBORAH

With a little shiver of dread.

Yes, I, too—

There is a pause during which they both stare straight before them. Their clasped hands, without their being aware, let go and draw apart. Each sneaks a suspicious, probing glance at the other. Their eyes meet and at once each looks away and forces a hypocritically affectionate, disarming smile. Deborah speaks quickly and lightly.

How quiet we are. What are you thinking, Daughter?

SARA

Quickly and lightly.

Of how foolish men can be, Mother, never content with what we give them, but always wanting more.

DEBORAH

Yes, they never grow up. They remain greedy little boys demanding the moon.

SARA

Getting up from the sofa.

I'll get my sewing, and come back to you.

DEBORAH

And I will read my book.

Sara goes slowly toward her old chair at left-front of table. Deborah's eyes remain fixed on her and abruptly her expression changes to one of arrogant disdainful repulsion and hatred. She thinks.

You vile degraded slut! As if you needed encouragement from me to become the vulgar grasping harlot you were born to be! But

I am glad I encouraged you because that is the one sure way to make him loathe the sight of you— In the end he will know you for what you are and you will so disgust him that he will drive you out of his life into the gutter where you belong!

> SARA
> *Having come to the chair, fiddles around unnecessarily gathering up her sewing things, keeping her back turned to Deborah, while she thinks.*

As if he'd waste his time in her crazy garden every evening, humoring her airs and graces, if she hadn't begged him to! But let her look out, I'll keep what's mine from her if I have to drive her into the asylum itself!

> *A pause. She stands motionless. Both their expressions change to a triumphant possessive tenderness.*

> DEBORAH
> *Thinking.*

Then my beloved son will have no one but me!

> SARA
> *Thinking.*

Then my darling will have only me!

> *She turns, making her face smilingly expressionless, and goes back toward the sofa. She sits down beside Deborah, and they smile a confidential smile at each other.*

CURTAIN

Act Three, Scene One

Scene Same as Scene One of Act Two—Simon's private office.
Changes have been made in its appearance. A sofa has
been added to the furniture. Placed at front-center, it is
too large for the room, too garishly expensive and luxu-
rious, in vulgar contrast to the sober, respectable conserv-
atism of the old office. A mirror in an ornate gilt frame
hangs over Sara's high desk at right-rear, and tacked on
the right wall beside her desk is a large architect's drawing
in perspective of a pretentious, nouveau-riche country
estate on the shore of a small lake, with an immense
mansion, a conglomerate of various styles of architecture,
as if additions had been made at different times to an
original structure conceived on the model of a mediaeval,
turreted castle.

It is early morning in mid-Summer of the following year,
1841.

SARA is discovered seated on the high stool before her
desk, working with a ruler and drafting instruments on a
plan. Her body has grown strikingly voluptuous and
provocatively female. She is dressed extravagantly in
flamboyant clothes. Her face has a bloated, dissipated
look, with dark shadows under her eyes. Her mouth
seems larger, its full lips redder, its stubborn character
become repellently sensual, ruthlessly cruel and greedy.
Her eyes have hardened, grown cunning and unscrupulous. Her manner varies between an almost masculine
curt abruptness and brutal frankness, plainly an imitation
and distortion of Simon's professional manner, and a
calculating feminine seductiveness.

The door from the bookkeeper's room at right is opened
noiselessly and JOEL HARFORD enters, closing the door
behind him. He is the same in appearance, retains the

*cold emotionless mask of his handsome face. But there is
a startling change in his manner, which now seems weak,
insecure, and furtive, as though he were thrown off
balance by some emotion he tries to repress, which
fascinates and at the same time humiliates him. For a
moment he stands glancing about the room vaguely, his
gaze avoiding Sara. She is conscious of his presence but
ignores him. Finally, seeing she is apparently absorbed
in her work, he stares up and down the curves of her
body with a sly desire.*

SARA

Suddenly explodes, slamming her rule on the desk.

Don't stand there gawking! How dare you come in here without
knocking? You know your orders! You better remember, if you
want to keep your job!

JOEL

Mr. Tenard, the banker, is in the outer office. I thought, considering his position, I had better announce him myself.

SARA

His position? His position now is under Simon's feet, and my feet!

JOEL

He states he had a letter from you making an appointment with
Simon.

SARA

What Simon wants of him I can't see. We've taken his bank from
him. Well, you see Simon's not here yet.

JOEL

My brother seems to be late every day now.

SARA

Forcing a too-careless tone.

Ah, he's taken to paying your old mother a morning visit in her
garden as well as in the evening.

Abruptly.

And what if he is late?

140

JOEL

As long as you don't mind his keeping *you* waiting.

SARA

Just what do you mean by that?

JOEL

Betraying an inner jealous excitability, his eyes fixed on the sofa—sneeringly.

I—I am not unaware why you are so insistent about my knocking before I—intrude.

SARA

Mockingly.

Well, that's my business.

JOEL

His eyes fixed fascinatedly on her now.

Your business! Yes, I quite realize you are—what you are.

SARA

Plainly enjoying this, moves her body seductively—teasingly.

And what am I, Joel darlin'?

JOEL

Trying to take his eyes from her.

I—I am fully aware of the means you have used in the past year to get my brother to sign over his interests one by one to you.

SARA

You don't think my love is worth it?

JOEL

I would not use the word love—

SARA

What else is love, I'm asking you?

JOEL

You pride yourself you have cunningly swindled him?

He laughs gratingly.

But it's you who have been swindled!

SARA

That's a lie!

JOEL

It was bad enough before you came here, but since he started playing Napoleon to show off his genius to you, he has abandoned all caution! If you had to pay the debts on the properties he has made over to you tomorrow—there would be nothing left! But once let his enemies see his true position—

SARA

Abruptly—frightened and shaken.

Oh, I know, Joel! Sometimes, I go mad worrying! But I can't stop him.

JOEL

It would take only a rumor—a whisper spoken in the right ear. This banker who is waiting—how he must hate Simon. If he had the slightest inkling—

SARA

I know.

Frightenedly.

You sound as though you'd like— You wouldn't—!

JOEL

I? Do you believe everyone is like you and Simon? Besides, you forget I still own an interest—which is not yet for sale, although I might consider—

SARA

Harshly.

Get back to your work! You're wasting my time and I'm sick of you!

She turns back to her desk.

JOEL

Moves mechanically to the door at right and is about to open it when suddenly he turns—angrily.

I do protest! —against you and my brother turning this office— my father's office—into a— Everyone is getting to know—to smirk and whisper! It is becoming an open scandal!

He stammers to a halt—his eyes fixed on her in helpless fascination. She has turned to him.

SARA
Smiling—teasingly.
Now, Joel darlin', you shouldn't look at me like that, and me your brother's wife.
She laughs.

JOEL
Fighting with himself.
I do not understand you. I do not see why you should laugh—like a common street woman.
He swallows as if he were strangling and tears his eyes from hers—stammers.
No, no! I do not mean— I do not recognize myself. I no longer recognize this as my father's office—or myself as my father's son. So please forgive and overlook—

SARA
Pitying and frightened.
Oh, don't I know! It's Simon. I've got to be what he wants. He makes me want to be what he wants! I forgive you, Joel. And please forgive me.

JOEL
I? Of course, Sara. And thank you for your kindness.
He turns to the door but again, with his hand on the knob, his eyes fix on her body and grow greedy.
I only wish to say—I've quite decided to sell my interest in the business—that is, to you, if you would care to consider—
He stops. She laughs teasingly. He wrenches open the door and flings himself into the bookkeeper's room, slamming the door behind him.

SARA
Looks after him and chuckles. She stares in the mirror at herself admiringly.
Who'd have dreamed it, Sara Melody—you in your beauty to have such power! By the Eternal, as my father used to swear, I think you could take what you wanted from any one of them!

*She suddenly shivers with repulsion and tears her eyes
from the mirror strickenly, in a guilty whisper.*

God forgive me! Me, to have such thoughts!

She stares around her frightenedly.

It's being here so long, with no life except in his greed— He's
made me think that life means selling yourself, and that love is
lust— It's only lust he wants—and he's made me feel it's all I
want and if I didn't have that hold on him, I'd lose him!—she'd
take him back with her entirely—

With angry defiance.

She'll never! I've only to kiss him and he forgets she's alive! And
what if I was having thoughts about Joel? He's a handsome man.
It was only what every woman thinks at times in her heart— Was
any one of us ever content with one man?

*She laughs—then suddenly tears her eyes from the mirror
and shrinks into herself with horrified disgust.*

Oh, God help me! I must be going daft—as daft as that mad old
witch in her garden.

She jumps from her stool.

Why doesn't he come? She keeps him dreaming in her garden to
make him late on purpose to torment me! And he lets her do it!—
Well, I won't wait, my fine Simon! Not alone!

*She is moving towards the bookkeeper's room when the
door from the rear is opened and* SIMON *comes in. He has
changed greatly, grown terribly thin, his countenance is
pale and haggard, his eyes deep sunken. There is, however, a strange expression of peace and relaxation on his
face as he enters, a look of bemused dreaminess in his eyes.
With a cry of happy relief, Sara rushes to him and hugs
him passionately.*

Oh, Darling! I love you so!

*Then her tension snapping she bursts into sobs and hides
her face against his shoulder.*

SIMON

*Startled and bewildered as if only half awakened from a
dream—pats her shoulder mechanically—vaguely.*

There, there.

He stares around him, thinking and frowning, as though not quite realizing yet where he is or how he got there.

SARA

Stops crying instantly at the tone of his voice, holds him by the shoulders, and stares into his face—frightened.

Simon! You sound—!

Forcing a joking tone.

For the love of Heaven, don't you know who I am?

SIMON

Trying to force himself from his day dream—vaguely placating.

Don't be silly.

He relapses and smiles dreamily.

Do you know, this morning, talking with Mother, I suddenly remembered something I had never remembered before. Nothing important. The astonishing thing is that she says I wasn't more than a year old at the time. Nothing important, as I've said. But it gave me a feeling of power and happiness to be able to recall the past so distinctly.

SARA

Stares at him—frightened and resentful.

Simon! Wake up! You're here with me!

She kisses him fiercely.

Come back to me! I love you! I'm your wife and you're mine. Tell me you love me.

SIMON

Awakes completely. His expression changes and he presses her body to his and kisses her passionately.

Sweetheart! You know I want you more than life!

SARA

With a sudden revulsion, pushes back from him.

No! I want love—

Then, forcing a laugh, she throws herself in his arms again.

Oh, I don't care as long as I have you!

SIMON

My dear beautiful mistress!
Tries to take her to the couch.

SARA

Breaks away from him. She laughs tantalizingly.
Oh no, you don't! You've a lot of business to attend to. You've got to earn me, you know!

SIMON

What do you want me to pay you this time? You have about all I possess already.

SARA

Well, there's the bank we've just got control of.

SIMON

Laughingly.
Oh, so that's it! I have had the papers drawn. But of course I won't sign them until after—

SARA

But how do I know you mightn't refuse to sign after—?

SIMON

Tries to draw her to him.
Darling! Haven't you learned by this time that my greatest happiness is to prove to you—and to myself—how much you are worth to me?

SARA

Coquettishly.
No, I said. Later.
She kisses him tantalizingly.
But here's a kiss to bind the bargain.

SIMON

But I have to run down to the mills today. There's been some discontent about our lowering wages and the hands are sending a deputation.

SARA

Fire them! There's plenty to take their place.

SIMON

I agree with you. But about our bargain. You said later, but I can't get back until late afternoon just in time for my evening visit with Mother. So—

SARA

Harshly domineering.
So you'll forget her and only remember me!

SIMON

Struggling to resist.
But I promised her—

SARA

You were late again this morning on account of seeing her. She did it on purpose! Ah, don't make excuses for her.

SIMON

Sharply matter-of-fact.
I've explained until I'm tired that I think it advisable, for our own sakes if not for hers, to humor her. And someone has to humor her and keep her from being too much alone in her fantastic mind—

SARA

I've told you before I'm willing to let her have the children for company again—

SIMON

Nonsense. I would never permit— She does not want your children now that she has—
    Abruptly changing the subject, going to his desk with his most alert authoritative executive air.
Well, I'll make up for lost time. Tenard is here, isn't he? You can tell Joel to have him sent in.

SARA

Her manner that of an efficient, obedient secretary.

Yes, Sir.

    She opens the door at right, sticks her head in and speaks to Joel, then comes back to the desk opposite Simon and waits for orders.

SIMON

I'll have time to dispose of him before I catch my train. You can go back to work on your plans for the estate.

She turns back toward the desk at right-rear. He glances at the plans—with an undercurrent of mockery.

Now that you'll soon possess a bank, too, you can afford to add still more. I am sure in your dreams you have already thought of more.

SARA

Oh, trust me, I can always think of more! Ah, won't it be a beautiful life, when I can sit back at my ease there, without a care in the world, watching my sons grow up handsome rich gentlemen, having my husband and my lover always by me and with no thought in his heart or brain but the great need to love me!

SIMON

Stares at her back—quietly, with a mocking irony tinged with a bitter, tragic sadness.

There is a poem by Doctor Holmes you should read sometime—for added inspiration.

He quotes from "The Chambered Nautilus."

"Build thee more stately mansions, O my soul,
        As the swift seasons roll!
        Leave thy low-vaulted past!
    Let each new temple, nobler than the last,
    Shut thee from heaven with a dome more vast,
        Till thou at length art free,
    Leaving thine outgrown shell—"

He pauses—then his gaze turned inward, he murmurs aloud to himself, as Sara continues to stare with fascinated, dreamy longing at the plan.

You must have that engraved over the entrance. And Mother should put it over the magic door to her summer-house. And I, on the ceiling of this Company's offices—in letters of gold!

There is a knock on the door at rear.

SARA

Her attitude becoming again that of the efficient secretary.

That must be Tenard, Sir. Shall I let him in?

SIMON

A strange, calculating gloating comes into his face.

No. I've just had an idea, Sara. Let Tenard wait outside the door for a while like the ruined beggar he is.

He gets up from his chair.

Come and sit in my place. I'd like to see you prove that, no matter what happened to me, you are fully competent to direct the destiny of this Company.

SARA

What could happen to you?

SIMON

Who knows? All men are mortal.

SARA

Don't say it, Darling.

SIMON

Or I might simply go away—for a long, much-needed rest.

SARA

With frightened jealous anger.

Ah, I know who put that in your mind! And I know she'd stop at nothing now to get you away with her!

SIMON

You've bought the Company, anyway, so—

SARA

Frightenedly.

You'd leave me—?

Coarsely self-confident.

I'd like to see you try to want to! Don't you know I've bought you, too?

There is another knock on the door, but neither heeds it.

SIMON

Yes, I know—and it is my greatest happiness to belong to you—to escape myself and be lost in you—I'll pay anything!

SARA

Laughs softly.

That's my Simon! That's the way I like you to talk—about life and love—and not about death.

SIMON
Starts toward her.

Beloved!

There is another knock on the door, sharp and impatient. Simon tears his eyes from Sara.

I think our friend is now sufficiently fearful and humiliated. Sit here, Sara. I am confident you can soon show him his place.

SARA
Comes to the desk—smiling gloatingly. She sits down in Simon's chair.

But I don't even know why you had him come, Simon. We've ruined him. He has nothing left we want, has he?

SIMON
Yes. A few years of his life. He's a capable banker and can still be useful to us. Not as he is now, of course. He is too full of old-fashioned ethics and honor. We know that because it made him so easy to ruin. If you can, discover his weakness and then use it without scruple. You will find a couple of notes I made on the pad about his present circumstances. The rest I leave in your capable hands, My Beautiful.

He laughs, moving away from her to her desk at right-rear. There is another, banging knock on the door. He calls curtly.

Come in!

The door is opened and BENJAMIN TENARD *enters. He is a tall, full-chested man in his sixties, with a fine-looking Roman face, his clothes expensively conservative. He has the look of success, of financial prosperity still stamped on him from long habit. This façade makes all the more pityingly acute the sense one immediately gets that he is a broken man inside. His face as he enters is flushed with humiliated pride.*

TENARD
See here, Harford! You made an appointment with me, not I

with you! Yet I am allowed to cool my heels in your outer office
and then stand outside your door knocking and knocking like
someone—!

> SARA
> *Breaks in—without any hint of apology.*

Sorry to have kept you waiting, Mr. Tenard.

> *He turns to stare at her in surprised confusion, not having
> noticed her at first.*

> TENARD

I—I beg your pardon, Mrs. Harford. I did not see—

> SARA
> *Nodding at the chair opposite her.*

Won't you sit down?

> TENARD
> *Uncertainly, glancing at Simon.*

Thank you.

> SIMON
> *Smiling with cold pleasantness.*

It's all right. Your appointment is really with my wife. So if you
will pardon me—

> *He nods at the plans on Sara's desk, turns his back on
> Tenard, and sits down. Tenard comes and sits in the
> chair opposite Sara.*

> SARA
> *After a quick glance at the pad.*

I presume you wonder why I wished to see you, Mr. Tenard. Just
as I was wondering why you ever consented to come—under the
circumstances.

> TENARD

You mean because your husband is responsible for ruining me?

> SARA

Simon does nothing without my consent, Mr. Tenard. I thought
that was the cheapest way to take possession of your bank.

TENARD

Yes, I have heard rumors that you advise him. I could not believe—
Then avoiding her eye and forcing a smile.
I bear no grudge. All is fair in war. Perhaps, I considered the methods used not quite ethical—not to say ruthless. There are some who would describe them in even stronger terms.

SARA

You owned something I desired. I was strong enough to take it. I am good because I am strong. You are evil because you are weak.

TENARD

An infamous credo, Madam!
Then almost cringingly.
I—I beg your pardon. You may be right. New times, new customs—and methods.
Forcing a laugh.
I suppose I am too old a dog to learn new tricks of a changed era.

SARA

I hope not—for your sake, Mr. Tenard.

TENARD

Eh? I don't believe I understand—
Hastily forcing a good-natured, good-loser air.
But, as I said, I have no hard feelings. That's why I consented to come here—

SARA

I know your true reason for coming. You haven't a dollar. But you have an old mother, a wife, a widowed daughter with two children. You have applied to various banks for a position. You are too old. The evil reputation of recent failure prejudices them against you. One or two have offered you a minor clerk's job— like a penny of charity tossed to a beggar.

TENARD

Yes, damn them! But I—

SARA

Moreover, the wage would have been insufficient to support your family except in a shameful poverty. You were afraid that your mother, your wife, your daughter, would begin to blame you for your weakness.

TENARD
Staring at her fascinatedly—blurts out in anguish.
That would be the worst! To feel them hiding it—out of pity.

SARA
But there was one last desperate hope. You heard I had not yet chosen anyone to manage your old bank for me. You came here hoping against hope that the reason I had sent for you—
She pauses—then smiles with cold pleasantry.
I am pleased to tell you that is the reason. Mr. Tenard, I do offer you that position.

TENARD
Gives way to relief and gratitude.
I—I don't know how to thank you—I apologize for having misjudged you— Of course, I accept the position gladly.

SARA
Wait! There are conditions. But before I state them, let me say that any sentiment of gratitude on your part is uncalled for. What happens to you and yours is naturally a matter of entire indifference to me. I am solely concerned with what is mine.

TENARD
You are—brutally frank, at least, Mrs. Harford. What are your conditions?

SARA
I warn you your pride will probably be impelled to reject them. The conditions are that you agree to obey every order mechanically, instantly, unquestioningly, as though you were the meanest worker in my mills.

TENARD
Humiliated, but forcing a reasonable tone.
You can rely on me; I have been the head of a business myself. I know the desirability of prompt obedience.

SARA

I can offer you a salary that will enable you to provide very moderate comfort for your family, and so continue to purchase, in part at least, their former love and respect.

TENARD

Stammers confusedly.

I— I thank you—

SARA

I am saying these things because, in order to avoid all future misunderstanding, I want you to face the cost of my offer before you accept.

TENARD

I understand. But you need not— I have no choice. I accept.

SARA

I hope you appreciate from your recent experience with my methods that you will have to forget all scruples. Where it is necessary, you must faithfully do things which may appear to your old conceptions of honor like plain swindling and theft. Are you willing to become a conscious thief and swindler?

TENARD

At last insulted beyond all prudent submission.

I— You must be mad, Madam— You dare—! But I cannot answer a woman— I know it must be your husband who—

He springs to his feet and turns on Simon in a fury.

Damn you, Sir! Do you think I have sunk to your level? I'd rather starve in the gutter like a dog! That's my answer to your infamous offer, Sir.

Simon has not turned, gives no sign of hearing him. Tenard grabs the handle of the door.

SARA

Suddenly bursts out—lapsing into broad brogue, forgetting all her office attitudes.

Arrah, God's curse on you for a man! You're pretending to love your women and children and you're willing to drag them down with you in the gutter, too!

TENARD

It's a lie! They would never wish me—

All at once he seems to collapse inside. He nods his head in a numbed acquiescence, forcing a vacant smile.

Yes, I suppose, entirely selfish—no time to remember self. Thank you, Madam, for reminding me of my duty. I wish to say I see your point about policy of bank—only practical viewpoint—business is business—

He forces a choked chuckle.

Must remember the old adage—sticks and stones—and poverty—break—but names don't hurt. Let who will cry thief! I accept the position, Madam—and thank you again—for your—charity!

He wrenches open the door and flings himself into the hall, slamming the door. Simon gets off his stool and comes to Sara.

SIMON

Well done! I'm proud of you.

SARA

Her expression is changing. There is a look of dawning horror in her eyes. She forces a smile—mechanically.

I'm glad you're proud. But it was you—what you wanted me—

SIMON

Oh, no. Don't play modest now. That last touch finished him, and that was all your own. I had calculated he would leave, but be forced to come back after he'd faced his women again. But your method was far cleverer.

He pats her shoulder.

SARA

Yes, I didn't leave him one last shred of his pride, did I?

She suddenly breaks—with a sob.

God forgive me!

Abruptly she turns on Simon—with rising bitter anger.

It wasn't I! It was you! Don't I know what you're trying to do, so you can go back and sneer with her at what a low, common slut I am in my heart!

Revengefully.

But I won't let you! I'll go to Tenard! He'll be crazy to revenge himself now! I've only to give him a hint of the true condition of the Company, and then where would you be, you and your Company? You'd not have a penny! And I'd be free to take my children and go to the old farm and live like a decent, honest woman working in the earth!

Sobbing, hiding her face in her hands.

I can't go on with this! I won't!

SIMON

Come now, Sara. I know you've just been under a severe strain.

With a strange tense excitement.

Of course you are right in thinking there is constant danger—that a whisper, a hint of the truth, a rumor started among the many defeated enemies who have such good reason to envy and hate you—

SARA

Reason to hate *me?*

SIMON

Well, do you imagine Tenard loves you, for example?

SARA

But it was you—

SIMON

There's no question about the danger. It's like walking a tight-rope over an abyss—

SARA

Oh, I know! It's driving me crazy! I can't sleep, worrying!

SIMON

But you mustn't look down, for then you grow confused and the temptation seizes you to hurl yourself— Don't you think I know how that impulse fascinates you, to make an end of suspense and gain forgetfulness and peace at any cost—to destroy oneself and be free!

SARA

Darling! Don't think of it! Don't make me think—

SIMON

I know only too well how tempted you are to whisper and start the rumor of the truth among your enemies—to throw off the burden of responsibility and guilt—not to have to go on! To be able to be still, or to turn back to rest!

He is staring before him with a fascinated yearning.

SARA

Frightened—grasping his arm.

Darling! Please don't stare like that! It makes you look so— strange and crazed—you frighten me!

SIMON

I? I was only warning you against it. You must not be weak. You must go on to more and more!

SARA

No. I don't want to. Oh, Simon darling, won't you be content now you've got the bank? Won't you let the profit add up, and pay off what you owe? And we'll pension off your mother, and give her the house to live alone in, and I'll build my estate and have a home of my own for my husband and my children—

She presses against him.

And best of all, for my lover.

SIMON

Ignoring this last—curtly.

The battle for this bank has strained your resources to the breaking point. A dollar in cash is worth a hundred to you now. No. You must go on.

SARA

Distractedly.

No! I can't! I've come to the end!

SIMON

You still have to have stores to retail your cotton goods— Your own plantations worked by your own slaves— Your own slave ships and your own slave dealers in Africa. That will complete the chain on the end. On this end, the stores are the last possible link— Of course, it would be the crowning achievement if I could conceive a scheme by which the public could be compelled to buy your cotton goods and only yours—so you would own your own consumer slaves, too. That would complete the circle with a vengeance! You would have life under your feet then, just as you have me!

He laughs, his eyes glowing with desire, and hugs her.

SARA

Her face lighting up—laughingly.

I'd be satisfied then. So see that you find a way to do it! Haven't I always said you've the strength and the power to take anything from life your heart wished for!

SIMON

With such an insatiable mistress to inspire me, how could I dare be weak? I could not respect myself unless you were proud of me.

SARA

And I am proud! I've the grandest, strongest lover that was ever owned by a woman!

She kisses him ardently.

Darling!

SIMON

Abruptly, with a matter-of-fact tone.

Well, that's settled.

He glances at his watch.

And now I'll have to go and catch my train.

He starts for the door. She gets in his way.

SARA

Leaving me without a kiss? When I'm making myself all you want me to be? Never mind! Be cruel to me! I'm dirt under your feet and proud to be! If it's a whore you love me to be, then I am it, body and soul, as long as you're mine!

She kisses him fiercely.

I want you! I can't bear you to leave me now! But you'll come back here. I'll be waiting and longing—

SIMON

Kisses her passionately.

Yes! I swear to you! Nothing could keep me from—

SARA

You won't forget me like you did this morning. You'll remember you promised me you'd forget her and let her wait.

SIMON

Let the cowardly old witch wait until Domesday! It will serve her right to be alone in the twilight she dreads so with her idiotic superstitious terror of the haunted summer-house!

He stops abruptly and his expression changes to bitter resentment.

What are you trying to do, eh? I had forgotten her! Why do you make me remember? Can't I be free of her even here in your arms? Why do you think I pay such an outlandish price to keep a mistress? Have you made a secret bargain with her to play one another's game? She never lets me forget you for long in her garden. She pretends to be jealous of you, just as you pretend— But I know you hate me more and have determined to get rid of me! But you had better not go on with your plot, because I warn you—it will be I who—

He checks himself, his eyes gleaming with a wild threat.

SARA

Staring at him—in a panic of dread.

Simon! Don't look like that! What's happened to you?

Suddenly resentful and angry herself.

God pity you for a fool! Play her game for her? When my one wish about her is to drive her away forever where she can never come back to steal what's mine—

SIMON

With a cold calculating sneer.

So you boast here behind her back, but with her you're afraid of her!

SARA

I, afraid of a poor old—!

SIMON

I will believe your boasting, Sara, when you prove you want me to be yours enough that you have the courage to—

In a burst of strange deadly hatred.

Are you going to let her come between us forever? Can't you rid our life of that damned greedy evil witch?

SARA
Stares at him with dread—but with a fascinated eagerness too. In a whisper.
You mean you want me to—?

SIMON
With a change to a lover's playful teasing—pats her cheek.
I want you to do anything in life your heart desires to make me yours. God knows I have paid you enough to prove it to you!
He laughs and kisses her.
I must catch my train. Goodbye until this afternoon.
He goes out rear. She stands looking after him, the same expression of horrified eagerness on her face.

CURTAIN

Act Three, Scene Two

Scene   *Same as Scene Two of Act Two—the corner of Deborah's garden with the summer-house. It is around nine o'clock the same night. There is a full moon, but clouds keep passing across it so that the light is a ghostly grey, in which all objects are indistinct and their outlines merge into one another, with intermittent brief periods of moonlight so clear the geometrical form of each shrub and its black shadow are sharply defined. Their alternating lights are like intense brooding moods of the garden itself, and it has more compellingly than ever before the atmosphere of a perversely magnified child's toy garden, distorted and artificial.*

DEBORAH *is discovered pacing back and forth along the path between the pool in front of the summer-house and the door to the street in the wall at right. One feels she is fighting back complete nervous collapse, wild hysterical tears. Yet at the same time she is a prey to a passionate anger and her eyes smoulder with a bitter, jealous hatred. A great physical change is noticeable in her. Her small, girlish figure has grown so terribly emaciated that she gives the impression of being bodiless, a little, skinny, witch-like, old woman, an evil godmother conjured to life from the pages of a fairy tale. Her small, delicate, oval face is haggard with innumerable wrinkles, and so pale it seems bloodless and corpse-like, a mask of death, the great dark eyes staring from black holes. She is dressed in white, as ever, but with pathetically obvious touches of calculating, coquettish feminine adornment. Her beautiful white hair is piled up on her head in curls so that it resembles an eighteenth-century mode. Her withered lips are rouged and there is a beauty-spot on each rouged cheek. There is an aspect about her of an old portrait of a bygone age come back to haunt the scene of long-past assignation.*

God, how long have I waited like this—hours!—hours since supper even—the children watching, their prying eyes sneering—mocking, snickering—but frightened, too— She has told them to beware of me, I am a little crazy— Then after supper out here again—waiting again— Why do I?—

> *She suddenly stops and listens, tensely—eagerly. She rushes over, pulls open the door in the wall at right, and looks out in the street—then closes it again—dully.*

No one—except Life, perhaps, who walks away again now— How many times now have I run to open the door, hoping each time—? How dare he humiliate me like this! You had better beware, Simon, if you think I will bear your insults without retaliating! No, no, I must not blame him— He has been detained at the mills— He loves me— He knows that his visits here are all that is left me— But if he had been detained at the mills, that does not explain why she has not returned home either— He must be with her!— He is even now lying in the arms of that slut, laughing with her to think of the pitiable spectacle I make waiting in vain! Oh why does she force me to hate her so terribly?— I know so well the scheme she has in mind to get rid of me—to drive me insane— She deliberately goads me!—but of course she hopes I would go alone—

> *She laughs sneeringly.*

Oh no, my dear Sara, I would take what is mine with me!

> *As she is speaking the moon comes from behind a cloud and shines clearly on the summer-house door. She stops and stares at it fascinatedly—then turns away hastily with a shiver of dread.*

No! I could not! —there is no need—I have encouraged him to make a whore of her—until now he sees her as the filthy slut she is—soon she will disgust him so he will drive her out of my house—meanwhile—

> *Her face has taken on a soft, dreamy, ecstatic look—exultantly.*

My beloved son and I—one again—happily ever after.

> *Her eyes fasten on the summer-house door again.*

Abruptly frightened, she turns away to stare about the garden uneasily.

If he would only come! I am afraid alone in this garden at night— It becomes strange—somber and threatening— And something in my nature responds—

She pauses—then with increasing bitterness and suspicion.

Why do I lie and tell myself it is I who have led Simon back into the past, when I know it is he who has forced me to carry out his evil scheme of revenge—? No!— How can I have such a mad suspicion? I should be glad— It proves how he loves me—how much he needs my love—

Suspiciously again—sneering at herself.

Love? You know he is incapable of love— Lust is the only passion he feels now—and the hate for me she has put in his mind—a conspiracy with her to drive me back further and further within myself—until he finally tricks me into unlocking the door, taking his hand— And at the last moment he will snatch his hand away, push me inside alone with that mad woman I locked in there—

The moon again comes from behind a cloud and shines on the summer-house. She gives a dreadful little laugh.

And then, of course, it would be so simple to have me locked up in an asylum— But take care, Simon! I will be the one to snatch away my hand and leave you alone in there with that old mad Deborah, who will have no scruple—and you beat the walls, screaming for escape at any cost!

She suddenly stops and presses her hands to her head torturedly.

Oh, God have mercy!— I must stop thinking— If I go on like this, there will be no need for anyone outside me to— I will drive myself in there!

She paces back and forth.

He has been detained— I must be patient—find some way to pass the time—I remember when I waited for him at the cabin that afternoon, I passed the time pleasantly in dreaming—and when I opened my eyes he was there—

She sits on the stone bench at right-rear of the pool, closing her eyes; her face grows tense as she concentrates her will, deliberately hypnotizing herself into a trance. She relaxes slowly and murmurs dreamily.

The gardens at Malmaison—the summer-house—the Emperor—

Her dream becomes disturbed, but she only half awakes.

No—I do not wish this—not Versailles and the King—the Emperor
Napoleon?—I had thought I hated him—Father's silly confusing
him with God—and Simon pretending he is like—

Sinking happily into dreams.

The Emperor kisses me—"My Throne, it is your heart, Dear
Love, and I—"

While she is saying this last, SARA *slinks in noiselessly
along the path from the house at left. She looks worn out
and dissipated, with dark circles under her eyes. She
stands regarding Deborah with a cruel mocking leer of
satisfaction. Deborah's face, in her dream, lights up.*

At last you have come, Sire. My poor heart was terrified you had
forgotten I was waiting.

Laughs softly and seductively, rising to her feet.

Give me your hand and let us go within, Sire—in our Temple of
Love where there is only beauty and forgetfulness!

*She holds out her hand and clasps that of her royal dream
lover, turns towards the door and slowly begins to ascend
the steps.*

I have the key here, Sire. I have worn it lately over my heart.

*She reaches down inside her bodice and pulls out a key
on a cord around her neck—hesitates frightenedly—then
unlocks, but does not open the door.*

I—I confess I am a little frightened, Sire. Oh, swear to me again
you would not deceive me—that it is love and forgetfulness!

SARA
Struggling with herself.

She knows, even in her dream!

DEBORAH
Forcing a determined, exulting tone.

But even if it were hell, it will be heaven to me with your love!

She puts her hand on the knob.

SARA

Yes, go to hell and be damned to you and leave Simon alone to me!

164

Then, just as Deborah is turning the knob, she springs toward her.

Stop! Let go of that door, you damned old fool!

Deborah starts and half-awakens with a bewildered cry, pulling her hand from the door, and stands dazed and trembling. Sara grabs her by the shoulders and shakes her roughly.

Wake up from your mad dreams, I'm saying!

DEBORAH

Whimpering like a child.

Let go! You are hurting me! It isn't fair! You are so much stronger! Simon! Make her let me alone!

Sara has let go of her. Deborah stares at her, fully awake now. She makes a shaken attempt to draw herself up with her old arrogance.

You! How dare you touch me!

SARA

I'm sorry if I hurt you, but I had to wake you—

DEBORAH

Oh, I'd like to have you beaten! Lashed till the blood ran down your fat white shoulders!

SARA

And that's the thanks I get for stopping you!

DEBORAH

How dare you come here!

SARA

To hell with your airs and graces! Whose property is it, I'd like to know? You're the one who has no right here!

DEBORAH

Oh!

SARA

I took pity on you, knowing you'd be kept waiting out here all night like an old fool, if I didn't tell you he'd come home with me and forgotten all about you.

DEBORAH

Then—it is true. He did go back to the office, instead of— You made him, with your filthy—!

SARA

Tauntingly.

Made him? I couldn't have kept him from me if I'd wanted!

DEBORAH

You came here to tell me—so you could gloat! You vulgar common slut!

SARA

And I've more to tell you. He's paid the last visit here he'll ever pay you. He swore to me on his honor, lying in my arms!

DEBORAH

You lie! He will come!

SARA

He'll never come here again, I'm telling you! So don't be dreaming and hoping! A filthy harlot, am I? Well, I'm what he loves me to be! What were you in your crazy dreams just now—?

DEBORAH

Shrinking back to the foot of the steps—guiltily.

No, no! Only in a silly fancy—to while away the time—

SARA

You don't fool me! It used to be King Louis of France. But now it's the Emperor Napoleon, God pity you! You've never enough! It'll be the Czar of Russia next!

DEBORAH

Shrinking back to the top step—distractedly.

Don't! Don't! Let me alone!

SARA

Following her.

Begging you to let them sleep with you! When out of your mad dreams you're only a poor little wizened old woman no common man on the street would turn to look at, and who, in the days when the men did want you, didn't have the strength to want them but ran and hid in her garden.

DEBORAH
With a pitiful, stammering, hysterical laugh.
Yes! So ridiculous, isn't it? So pitiful and disgusting and horrible! Don't! Don't make me see! I can't endure myself! I won't! I'll be free at any cost! I—
She turns and grabs the knob of the door.

SARA
Instinctively makes a grab for her and pulls her away— covering her guilty fear with a rough anger.
Come away from that!

DEBORAH
No! Let me go!

SARA
You will, will you?
She picks Deborah up in her strong arms, as if she weighed nothing, sets her down before the bench at right and forces her down on it.
Sit there and be quiet now! If you think you'll make me have your madness on my conscience, you're mistaken!
Deborah crumples up and falls sideways face down on the bench and bursts into hysterical sobbing.
Ah, thank God, you can cry. Maybe that will bring some sense back in your head.
Her tone becomes more and more persuasive as Deborah's crying gradually spends itself.
I've told you the truth. Simon swore he'd never come to you again. It was part of the price I made him pay for me when he came back from the mills. He's mine now! He's paid me everything he has. He has nothing left but me and my love. I'm mother, wife, and mistress in one. He doesn't need you, Deborah.
Deborah is still now and listening tensely, but she does not raise her head.
The real reason I came here was to have a sensible talk with you. If you'll swear to stop your mad schemes, I'll make peace with

167

you. And I'll give the children back to you to keep you company and you'll be as contented as you were before. And I won't hate you. You know I don't like your forcing me to hate you, don't you?

She pauses. Deborah remains still. Sara's anger rises.

Haven't you a tongue in your head? It's you, not me, ought to beg for peace!

DEBORAH

Abruptly straightens up and stares at her—with a mocking smile.

You are even more stupid than I thought. Don't you know your begging for peace is a confession of how insecure you are in your fancied victory? You realize that any time I choose I can take Simon away with me!

SARA

Frightenedly.

You mean, into madness, with you? I swear by Almighty God I'll murder you if you try that.

DEBORAH

Coldly disdainful.

And get your children's mother hanged?

SARA

I'll do it a way no one will discover!

DEBORAH

Simon would know. Do you think your husband would love a wife who had murdered his mother?

SARA

He'd thank me for it!

DEBORAH

You lie! He loves me! It's you he hates. He loathes your foul flesh, your filthy, insatiable greeds!

SARA

Ah, it's the evil liar you are! He loves me!

DEBORAH

You stopped me from opening the door. You could really have won then but you are weakly sentimental and pitiful. You will always defeat yourself at the last.

SARA

You old lunatic, you'll see if I have any pity on you the next time!

DEBORAH

Haughtily—as if addressing a servant.

You have no business in this garden. Will you be good enough to return to the house where you belong and attend to your children? I know my son is waiting for an opportunity to see me alone.

SARA

Angrily, turning toward the path off left.

He's waiting, hoping to hear I've found you locked inside there and we can get the asylum to take you away!

DEBORAH

With a pitiful frightened cry.

Sara! No!

She runs to her wildly and grabs her arm—stammering with terror.

Don't go! Don't leave me alone, here! I—I'm afraid! Please stay! I—I'll do anything you ask! I'll promise anything you want! Only—don't leave me here!

She throws her arms around Sara and begins to sob hysterically.

Oh, how can you be so cruel to me?

SARA

Has stared at her at first suspiciously—then gloating triumphantly but moved in spite of herself—finally, as Deborah weeps, she is overcome by pity and soothes her as she would a child.

There, there now. Don't be frightened. I'm strong enough for the two of us. We won't destroy each other any more. You'll have the children back. You'll be happy and contented. Come in

169

the house with me now. It's a wonder if you haven't caught your death already, chilled by the night and the dew. Come.

DEBORAH

You are so thoughtful and good.
> *Sara begins to lead her off left. Abruptly she stops—with dread.*

No. We're forgetting he is there, Sara. We can't face him yet. We would be too weak. We must stay here together, trusting each other, until we get back our old strength—the strength his evil jealous greed has corrupted and destroyed. Yes, it is he! He! Not us! We have been driven to this!

SARA

> *Resentfully.*

Ah, don't I know how he's driven me!

DEBORAH

He! He! Only he! We saw that so clearly when he first started to goad us into this duel to the death! We swore to each other that we would constantly bear in mind it was he, not us.

SARA

I know! But he made us deceive each other and hate and scheme—

DEBORAH

How could we be so blind and stupid!

SARA

Because we loved him so much! And didn't he know that, and use it!

DEBORAH

We could have defeated him so easily! We would have been so much stronger!

SARA

And he'd have been happy and content.

DEBORAH

But instead we let him revive a dead hate of the past to start us clawing and tearing at each other's hearts like two mad female animals he had thrown in a pit—while he stands apart and watches and sneers and laughs with greedy pride and goads each on—!

SARA

And when only one is left living, he knows she'll never have strength to claim her body or soul her own again!

> *While she is talking, unnoticed by them both,* SIMON *appears behind them, entering from the path at left. He stands staring at them. He is in a state of terrific tension, and there is a wild look in his eyes, calculating and threatening and at the same time baffled and panic-stricken.*

DEBORAH

It would serve him right if we turned the tables on him, Sara. We could have the strength now as we are united again as one woman.

SARA

You mean, throw him in the pit—to fight it out with himself?

DEBORAH

For our love—while we watched with gratified womanly pride and laughed and goaded him on!

SARA

Until—

DEBORAH

Yes, Sara. Until at last we'd finally be rid of him. Oh God, think of how simply contented we could be alone together with our children—grandmother and mother, mother and daughter, sister and sister, one woman and another, with the way so clear before us, the meaning of life so happily implicit, the feeling of living life so deeply sure of itself, not needing thought, beyond all torturing doubt, the passive "yes" welcoming the peaceful procession of demanding days!

> *She pauses—then a bit guiltily.*

I hope you do not think it evil of me that I can find it in myself to wish he were not here.

SARA

There have been times at the office when I—

He has taught us that whatever is in oneself is good—that whatever one desires is good, that the one evil is to deny oneself. It is not us but what he has made us be! So on his head—

SIMON

With a tense casualness.

You are mistaken, Mother.

> *They both whirl on him with startled gasps of terror and cling to one another defensively. Then as he advances, they shrink back to the edge of the bench at the right-rear of pool, keeping the pool between them and him.*

I have merely insisted that you both be what you are—that what you are is good because it is fact and reality— What is evil is the stupid theory that man is naturally what we call virtuous and good—instead of being what he is, a hog. It is that idealistic fallacy which is responsible for all the confusion in our minds, the conflicts within the self, and for all the confusion in our relationships with one another, within the family particularly, for the blundering of our desires which are disciplined to covet what they don't want and be afraid to crave what they wish for in truth. In a nutshell, all one needs to remember is that good is evil, and evil, good.

> *As they have listened, the faces of the two women have hardened into a deadly enmity.*

DEBORAH

Do you hear, Sara? We must not forget.

SARA

No, we owe it to him to be what he wants.

SIMON

His tense quiet beginning to snap.

But I did not come out here to discuss my meditations on the true nature of man.

> *He pauses, then blurts out in violent accusation.*

I—I was trying to concentrate my thoughts on the final solution of the problem. I have been forced to the conclusion lately that in the end, if the conflicting selves within a man are too evenly matched—if neither is strong enough to destroy the other before

the man himself is in danger of being torn apart between them—
then that man is forced at last, in self-defense, to choose one or
the other—

Starts—staring at him uneasily.
To choose?

SARA
To choose?

SIMON
That appears to me now to be the one possible way he can end
the conflict and save his sanity.

DEBORAH
You hear what he's confessing, Sara? He is much nearer the end
than I had thought.

SARA
Yes, we've only to wait and we'll soon be free of him.
Scornfully resentful.
So he'll choose, will he, the great man? Like a master picking
which of two slaves he'd like to own! But suppose they don't
choose to let him choose?

DEBORAH
All they have to do is to wait together and stand apart and watch
while he destroys himself.
She laughs softly and Sara laughs with her.

SIMON
With an abrupt change to his matter-of-fact tone.
I don't know what you're talking about, Mother. I attempt to
explain an abstract problem of the nature of man, and you and
Sara begin talking as if you, personally, were directly concerned
in it!
He chuckles dryly.
An amusing example of the insatiable ambition of female posses-
siveness, don't you think?
Curtly.

Never mind. It is my fault for being such a fool as to discuss it with you. I know the one problem that interests you.

He becomes angrily excited.

God knows I could hardly be unaware of it tonight! I heard you from my study quarreling out here, clawing and tearing at each other like two drunken drabs. Do you want to create a public scandal, cursing and threatening each other?

DEBORAH

You could not possibly have heard us in your study. What you heard were the voices of your own mind.

SIMON

I heard you as clearly as if I were here! It seemed there would never be a moment's peace in my life again—that you would go on with your horrible duel, clawing and tearing each other, until my mind would be ripped apart! Are you trying to insinuate I am going insane? Ridiculous! I heard you, I tell you. And then when you finally did become quiet, it was the stillness that follows a shriek of terror, waiting to become aware— I was afraid one of you here—

DEBORAH

Staring at him—cannot control a shudder.

We know—you have been hoping—

SARA

Ah, God forgive you!

SIMON

Wildly.

Well, I might have been hoping. Suppose I was? Do you think I can endure living with your murderous duel forever—a defenseless object for your hatred of each other—rent in twain by your tearing greedy claws?

He suddenly breaks and sinks on the bench at left of pool, his head clutched convulsively in his hands—brokenly.

Why can't you stop? I will do anything you wish! Is there no love or pity left in your hearts? Can't you see you are driving me insane?

He begins to sob exhaustedly—the two women sit to-

gether, as one, on the other bench, staring at him, exhausted and without feeling.

DEBORAH
Dully.
We have won, Sara.

SARA
Yes, Deborah. He admits he's beaten.
They stare at him. Suddenly their faces, as one face, are convulsed by pitying, forgiving maternal love.

DEBORAH
Our poor boy! How could we be so cruel!

SARA
Our poor darling! How could we feel as we were feeling about you!
As one, they spring to their feet and go to him, separating, one coming round one side of the pool, the other round the other. They kneel at each side of him, putting an arm around him, hastening to console and comfort him.

DEBORAH
There, there! Our beloved son!

SARA
Our husband! Our lover!

DEBORAH
You mustn't cry, Dear.

SARA
There's nothing need frighten you now. We've forgiven you.

SIMON
Raises his head, a confused, dreamy wondering peace in his face—dazedly.
Yes. It is very restful here. I am very grateful to you.
He turns to Sara.
I love you, my mother.
He turns to Deborah.
I love you, my—

> *He stops guiltily—then springs from their arms to his feet, stammering distractedly.*

No, no! If you think I can be taken in by such an obvious sham—

> *The two women spring to their feet. Both cry as one: "Simon!" and each grabs one of his arms and clings to it. Simon trembles with his effort to control himself. He speaks with hurried acquiescence.*

I ask your pardon. My mind is still extremely confused. It is such an unexpected shock—to find Sara here where she never intrudes— and then to hear of your reconcilement— But it is my dearest wish—

SARA

Darling!

> *She hugs his arm.*

DEBORAH

Dear!

> *She kisses his cheek.*

SIMON

Thank you, Mother. Well, all is forgotten and forgiven, is that it?

DEBORAH

Oh yes, Dear! And we will make you so happy! Won't we, Sara?

SARA

Indeed we will! He won't know himself!

SIMON

Let us sit down and rest for a moment together then, in this garden so hidden from the ugliness of reality.

> *As they are about to sit, he suddenly exclaims.*

Ah, what a fool I am! I came to remind you, Sara, it's the children's bedtime and they are waiting for your goodnight kiss.

SARA

Ah, the poor darlings!

SIMON

> *With a calculating insistence.*

You'd better take a good look at Honey. It seemed to me he was a bit feverish.

SARA

Ah, the poor lamb!
She starts off the path at left, then hesitates.
You're coming in?

DEBORAH
Quickly.
Yes, of course—

SIMON

Yes, it's too damp and chilly. We'll go in, Mother. But you better run ahead, Sara, and see Honey.

SARA

Ah, I hope he's not going to be sick. I'll—
She hurries off, left. Simon turns and stares at his mother.

SIMON
With a sneering chuckle.
Well, you must admit I got rid of her very successfully. She will not notice we have remained out here.

DEBORAH
Stiffening—coldly.
I am not remaining here.

SIMON
Ignoring this.
It will give us an opportunity to be alone.

DEBORAH
I am going in and help her with the children. At once!
She takes a step towards left, stiffly, as if by a determined effort of will, staring at him with a fascinated uneasiness. He reaches out and takes one of her hands and she stops, trembling, rooted to the spot. She stammers.
You—you may do as you please. If you choose to stay out here alone in the darkness—dreaming childish make-believe—you, a grown man! Will you kindly let go my hand? I wish to go in and join Sara.

SIMON

Quietly.

What has your race and fastidious, dreaming poet's soul in common with that female animal?

DEBORAH

It is despicable of you to speak like that about a woman who loves you so deeply.

SIMON

You are speaking of my mistress. She made me pay two-fold the value of every pound of flesh— All I want now is to get rid of her forever.

DEBORAH

Struggling with herself.

No! You do not fool me! It is she who is tired of you. Good heavens, what woman wouldn't be disgusted with the greedy, soulless trader in the slave market of life you have become—!

Vindictively.

We will give you the freedom you used to dream about!

SIMON

Tensely.

Oh, if you knew how desperately I long to escape her and become again only your son!

DEBORAH

Oh, how can you lie like that? —when you deliberately kept me waiting here hour after hour—while you lay in her arms— Ah, how I hated you! How I cursed the night you were conceived, the morning you were born!

SIMON

What could I do? She is so beautiful and she demanded it as part of her price. And you must remember that there, with her, my life lives in her life, and hers in mine, and I am her Simon, not yours. So how could I wish to remember you?

DEBORAH

Tensely—making a futile movement to rise.

And you think that excuses—?

SIMON

Just as here with you now, as always in the past before she intruded—
Goes on in the same tone of tense quiet.
You know her true nature well enough to realize it was she who made me laugh with her in her arms to think of you waiting here like an old fool—

DEBORAH
In a deadly fury.
I could hear her! The infamous harlot! But there will be no peace as long as we both remain alive!
She stops frightenedly.

SIMON

If someone stumbled and fell against her when she was starting to descend the steep front stairs, if—

DEBORAH
In a shuddering whisper.
Simon!

SIMON
Yes, I agree that is too uncertain.

DEBORAH
Stammers in confused horror.
Agree? But I never—!

SIMON
Poison would be certain. And no one would ever suspect anything but natural illness in an eminent, wealthy family like ours.

DEBORAH
Simon! Good God in heaven, have you gone mad?

SIMON
No. Quite the contrary. I am being extremely sane. I am alive to life as it is behind our hypocritical pretences and our weak sentimental moral evasions of our natural selves. I am not frightened by the bad names we have called certain acts, which in themselves are perfectly logical—the killing of one's enemies, for example. Our whole cowardly moral code about murder is but another example of the stupid insane impulsion of man's petty vanity to

believe human lives are valuable, and related to some God-inspired meaning. But the obvious fact is that their lives are without any meaning whatever—that human life is a silly disappointment, a liar's promise, a perpetual in-bankruptcy for debts we never contracted, a daily appointment with peace and happiness in which we wait day after day, hoping against hope, and when finally the bride or the bridegroom cometh, we discover we are kissing Death.

DEBORAH

No! Stop!

SIMON

Or, obsessed by a fairy tale, we spend our lives searching for a magic door and a lost kingdom of peace—

DEBORAH
Suddenly taunting.
Ah, if you are going to start harping on that childish nonsense—

SIMON

And when we find it we stand and beg before it. But the door is never opened. And at last we die and the starving scavenger hogs of life devour our carrion!

DEBORAH

Simon! Don't look like that! You frighten me!

SIMON
Quietly again.
Regarded sensibly, we should all have clauses in our wills expressing gratitude to, and suitably rewarding, anyone who should murder us. The murderer possesses the true quality of mercy.
He chuckles sardonically.
So, although I know how you have always, at any cost, escaped confronting facts—

DEBORAH
With strange scorn.
You are a fool! As if I did not once think exactly as you have been thinking.

SIMON

So I cannot see why the thought should make you shudder now.

DEBORAH

But those were dreams. Now it becomes real—when you put it in my mind. It begins to live in my will. It is born. It begins to be, to direct itself toward a consummation. And one day soon I will be hating her young body and her pretty face, and I will follow her to the top of the stairs—! Or I will remember that the gardener keeps arsenic in the cellar for killing vermin—!

Deliberately jumping to her feet.

You are insane! I am afraid to be alone with you!

Pulling at her hand.

Let me go! I will call Sara!

She calls.

Sara! Sara!

SIMON

Keeps hold of her hand—quietly.

She cannot hear.

He pulls her gently back—quietly.

Come. Sit down, Mother. What have you and I to do with her—?

Deborah weakly lets herself be pulled down beside him.

Can't you see I am trying to make clear to you that I have chosen you?

DEBORAH

Her face lighting up with a passionate joy.

You mean—you really mean—? Oh, I knew! I knew in the end I could not fail! Oh, my son! My beloved son!

Then frightened.

But not murder— You must not murder— Promise me you will not—

SIMON

No. There is another way. We will leave her here. We will go together so far away from the reality that not even the memory of her can follow to haunt my mind. You have only to open that door—

His eyes fasten on the summer-house door with a fasci-nated longing.

DEBORAH

Stares at it with dread and longing herself—forcing a belittling tone.

Now, Dear, you mustn't start harping on that fantastic childish nonsense again!

SIMON

I have waited ever since I was a little boy. All my life since then I have stood outside that door in my mind, begging you to let me re-enter that lost life of peace and trustful faith and happiness! You once drove me out, and all that has happened since began. Now you must either choose to repudiate that old choice, and give me back the faith you stole from me, or I will choose her!

DEBORAH

No!

SIMON

And then there will be no choice left to you but to run and hide in there again, and dream yourself into the madhouse to escape yourself!

DEBORAH

Horrified.

Simon! For God's sake, how can you say such things to your mother who loves you more than life! As if you wished—

SIMON

I wish to be free, Mother!—free of one of my two selves, of one of the enemies within my mind, before their duel for possession destroys it. I have no longer any choice but to choose. Or would you prefer I should go insane—and so be rid of me again?

DEBORAH

Shuddering.

No! Oh, how can you say—? You must be insane already—!

SIMON

Coldly.

You are compelling me to choose her.

He lets go her hand.

Very well. I shall go to her. Do not attempt to follow me. I shall

182

lock you out as you once did me. You will stay here alone until
you do what you must do to escape. I have no doubt you will
find happiness in a foolish dream as a King's courtesan! And I
shall be free to be Sara's, body and soul. Goodbye, Mother.

He turns to go.

DEBORAH
Grabs his hand—pleading frantically.
No! For God's sake! I will do anything you ask.
*She leads him a step towards the door—then falters and
begins to argue desperately as if she were trying to con-
vince a child.*
But—you, a grown man—to make into a literal fact—an old
fairy story I made up in an idle moment to make you laugh!

SIMON
You know that is a lie, Mother! To make me realize you hated
your love for me because it possessed you and you wanted to
be free!

DEBORAH
But to connect the door and that silly tale with the actual wooden
door—that really is insane, Simon.

SIMON
Tensely.
I know very well it is a wooden door— But in the deeper reality
inside us, it has the meaning our minds have given it. Your opening it will be the necessary physical act by which your mind wills
to take me back into your love, and become again the mother
who loved me alone, whom alone I loved!
He smiles at her with a sudden awkward tenderness.
So you see it is all perfectly rational and logical, and there is
nothing insane about it, Mother. The kingdom of peace and
happiness in your story is love. You dispossessed yourself when
you dispossessed me. Since then we have both been condemned
to an insatiable greed for substitutes—
He stares obsessedly at the door again.
But you have only to open that door, Mother—really a door in
your own mind—

DEBORAH
With a shudder.
I know!—and I know only too well the escape it leads to!

SIMON
Pats her hand—tenderly persuasive, but his eyes fixed on the door.
Forget those silly fears, Mother. We have gone back before they existed, before Sara existed in me and I in her. We are back here in your garden on the day you told me that story.
He pauses—then turns on her with a bitter vindictive condemnation.
I have never forgotten the anguished sense of being suddenly betrayed, of being wounded and deserted and left alone in a life in which there was no security or faith or love but only danger and suspicion and devouring greed! By God, I hated you then! I wished you dead! I wished I had never been born!

DEBORAH
With an obviously fake air of contrition thinly masking a cruel satisfaction.
Did you, Dear? I am sorry if I hurt you. It is true I hoped you would guess what I meant. You were such a stubborn greedy little boy. I could feel your grasping fingers groping toward every secret, private corner of my soul. So I had to do something to warn you, and I thought a fairy tale—
Abruptly her expression changes to one of horror for herself—distractedly.
No! I never meant—! You put it in my mind! It's insane of you to make me confess such horrible things! And how can you admit you hated your mother and wished her dead!

SIMON
Passionately.
All I ask is that you go back and change that—change the ending—open the door and take me back— There will be only you and I! There will be peace and happiness to the end of our days! Can't you believe me, Mother? I tell you I know.

DEBORAH

Staring at the door fascinatedly.

Oh, if I could, Dear! If I only could believe! If you knew how desperately I have longed to have you back, to know you were mine alone. Yes! I believe now—believe that if the mind wills anything with enough intensity of love it can force life to its desire, create a heaven, if need be, out of hell!

SIMON

God, if the reality of dog-eat-dog and lust-devour-love is sane, then what man of honorable mind would not prefer to be considered lunatic! Come, Mother! Let us leave this vile sty of lust and hatred and the wish to murder! Let us escape back into peace—while there is still time!

DEBORAH

With forced eagerness, mounts the first step.

Yes—before I can think— Come, Dear.

SIMON

We shall have gone back beyond separations. We shall be one again.

Suddenly in a panic.

But hurry, Mother! Hurry! I hear someone coming!

Deborah moves so that she stands protectingly before Simon, her right hand on the knob of the door. Sara comes hurrying in from the left. She is in a panic of apprehensive dread. When she sees them both still outside the summer-house, this changes to rage against Deborah.

SARA

To Deborah.

You liar! You thief! You traitor! I should have known better than to leave you— But God be praised I'm back in time!

DEBORAH

Jeering quietly.

Yes. You are just in time—to bid us farewell!

SARA

Simon! Come here! Do you want to lose what little wits you've left?

> *But Simon appears not to have heard her, or to have noticed her coming. He keeps behind his mother, turned sideways to Sara, his eyes fixed fascinatedly on the door.*

DEBORAH

> *Addressing him over her shoulder her eyes on Sara.*

My love, you no longer remember this woman, do you?

SIMON

> *Turns his head to stare at Sara without recognition. His face has a strange, mad, trance-like look. He murmurs obediently.*

No, Mother.

> *He addresses Sara.*

How dare you trespass here? Do you think my mother's garden is a brothel?

SARA

> *Shrinks as if she'd been struck—strickenly.*

Simon! Don't speak like that— It is mad you are!

SIMON

> *Disdainfully.*

Begone! Before I summon the police!

> *Pointing to the door in the wall at right.*

That door leads to the street. Go back and ply your trade there.

SARA

Darling! It's I! Your Sara!

DEBORAH

> *Gloating—haughtily.*

You have my son's orders!

> *To Simon.*

But I think, Dear, it might be simpler for us to leave her now.

SIMON

> *Eagerly.*

Yes, Mother. Let us go!

186

DEBORAH
Exultantly.

Yes! I can now! I will take what my whim desires from life, and laugh at the cost!

> She laughs and with an abrupt movement jerks open the door behind her so it stands back against the wall. Simon gives a gasping eager cry and leans forward, staring into the darkness inside. But Deborah does not turn to it and remains confronting Sara.

SARA
Wildly.

No!

> Rushes up and grabs Deborah's skirt and falls on her knees before her.

For the love of God have pity, Deborah!

DEBORAH

Pity? Would you remind me of pity now, you scheming slut?

SARA
Pleadingly.

I'm asking your pity for him, not for me! You love him! You can't do this!

DEBORAH

Love is proud, not pitiful! Let go!

> She kicks her skirt from Sara's hand and half turns to the door, grabbing Simon's arm.

Come, Dear! Quick! Let us go where we cannot hear her lies about love and pity!

SIMON
Turns his head a little from staring inside the summer-house—dazedly and uneasily.

Who are you talking to, Mother? What is she trying to make me remember? This is long before any other woman.

DEBORAH
Cruelly scornful and at the same time uneasy.

Yes, I will not listen to her pleading lies! We will go—

187

SARA

Wildly, grabbing Deborah's skirt again.

No! Wait! Listen, Deborah! I give up! I admit I'm beaten now!

Throws herself forward and flings her arms around Deborah's legs—pleading.

Deborah! You can't! You can have him back! I'll go away! I'll never trouble you again! And that's all you've wanted, isn't it?

DEBORAH

Stares at her, unable to believe her ears.

You really mean—you will give up—go away—?

SARA

I will—for love of him—to save him. I'll sign everything over to you. All I'll keep is the old farm, so I'll have a home for my children, and can make a living with them. I'll take them there tomorrow.

She gets to her feet slowly and exhaustedly.

SIMON

He has remained tense and motionless, staring into the darkness inside the summer-house. In a boyish uneasy whisper, tugging at Deborah's hand.

Why are you waiting, Mother? We mustn't wait—or it may be too late!

But neither woman seems to hear.

SARA

You know no woman could love a man more than when she gives him up to save him!

DEBORAH

Sneeringly.

How shamelessly humble you are!

SARA

If I'm humbled, it's by myself and my love, not by you. I can wish him happiness without me, and mean it! Yes, and I can even wish you to be happy so you can make him happy!

DEBORAH

With strange repressed fury.

I begin to see your scheme—you want to make me feel con-
temptible—

SARA
Quietly and exhaustedly.
I've told you I'm beyond scheming. I'll leave you now, Deborah.
I'll get the children up now and take them to a hotel where he
can't find us. Give him a good excuse to give himself to forget
me. That's all he needs to bring him peace with you alone.
*She turns to go off left—brokenly, without looking at
Simon.*
God bless you, Simon, Darling, for all the joy and love you gave
me, and give you peace and happiness!

SIMON
With a sort of bewildered anguish.
Mother! Someone is calling me! I cannot remain back here much
longer! Hurry, Mother!

SARA
Goodbye, Deborah.
She starts to walk away.

DEBORAH
Sara—wait—forgive— I want to say—my gratitude—want to tell
you—you are beautiful and fine—so much more fine—than I—
Bursting into a jealous fury, glaring at her with hatred.
Damn you! You the noble loving woman! I the evil one who
desires her son's life! As if a low lustful creature like you could
even imagine the depth of the love I have for him! But I'll prove
to you who is the final victor between us, who is the one who
loves him most!
She turns to face the darkness within the doorway.

SIMON
With an eager cry.
Mother! At last!

SARA
Frightenedly.
Simon!

DEBORAH

Pulls her hand violently from his.

No! Alone!

SIMON

Despairingly—grabbing at her hand.

Mother!

DEBORAH

Flings his hand away—with a strange boastful arrogance.

Alone, I said! As I have always been! As my pride and disdain have always willed I be! Do not dare to touch me! Get back to the greasy arms of your wife!

With extraordinary strength she gives him a push in the chest that drives him off balance and sends him spinning down the steps to fall heavily and lie still by the stone bench at left of pool. She turns and stops on the threshold, confronting the darkness—with a self-contemptuous laugh.

To think you were afraid, Deborah! Why, what is waiting to welcome you is merely your last disdain!

She goes in quietly and shuts the door.

SARA

Has flung herself on her knees beside Simon and raised his head, oblivious to Deborah's going.

Darling! Are you hurt bad? Simon! Merciful God! Speak to me, Darling!

In a panic she puts her hand over his heart—relieved.

No, he's only fainted.

She begins to chafe his wrists.

Maybe it's best. He'd be trying to get in there.

She stops rubbing his wrists and turns to stare at the summer-house—in an awed, horrified whisper.

God help me, she's done it! Ah, it's a great noble lady you couldn't help proving yourself in the end, and it's you that beat me, for your pride paid a price for love my pride would never dare to pay!

She shudders.

I see now the part my greed and my father's crazy dreams in me had in leading Simon away from himself until he lost his way and began destroying all that was best in him! To make me proud of him! Ah, forgive me, Darling! But I'll give my life now to setting you free to be again the man you were when I first met you—the man I loved best!—the dreamer with a touch of the poet in his soul, and the heart of a boy!

With an almost masochistic satisfaction.

Don't I know, Darling, the longing in your heart that I'd smash the Company into smithereens to prove my love for you and set you free from the greed of it! Well, by the Eternal, I'll smash it so there'll be nothing left to tempt me! It's easy. It needs only a whisper of the true condition to Tenard, now he's in the Company.

With a gloating smile.

I can hear the revenge in his heart laughing, rushing out to tell all our enemies and combine with them to pounce down and ruin us! Well they can't take the old farm anyway, and we'll live there, and the boys will work with me, and you can write poetry again of your love for me, and plan your book that will save the world and free men from the curse of greed in them!

She pauses guiltily.

God forgive me, I'm happy at the mere thought of it, and it's no price at all I'll be paying to match yours, Deborah.

With an abrupt change to practical calculation.

That reminds me, before I start the whisper, I'll get all the Company's cash from the banks and put it in her name, along with this house, with Joel to take care of it, so she'll have enough and plenty to keep her here, with her garden, and the comfort and riches and luxury that's due the great Princess on her grand estate she'll be in her dream till the day she dies!

> *While she has been saying this last, the door of the summer-house has slowly opened and Deborah has appeared. She now stands on the top of the steps. Her eyes have a still, fixed, sightless, trance-like look, but her face is proud, self-assured, arrogant and happy. She looks beautiful and serene, and many years younger.*

DEBORAH

In a tone of haughty command.

Who is talking? How dare you come here?

SARA

Starts and stares at her—in an awed whisper.

Ah, God pity her, the poor woman!

DEBORAH

Coming down the steps— As she does so, Sara gets to her feet, letting Simon's head rest back on the grass. A look of recognition comes over her face—with a regal gracious condescension.

Ah, you are the Irish kitchen maid, are you not?

Approaching her, erect and arrogant and graceful, her head held high.

What are you doing in the Palace grounds at this hour? Do you not know there is a terrible punishment for trespassing in my domain?

SARA

Humoring her—bobs her an awkward servant-girl curtsy and speaks humbly.

I know I have no right here, My Lady.

DEBORAH

This garden is the Emperor's gift to me.

With a gloating little laugh. Then suddenly—sharply and suspiciously.

Why are you silent? Do you dare to doubt me?

SARA

Indeed I don't, Your Majesty.

DEBORAH

Reassured and pleasant.

I am not Majesty, my poor woman. Of course, if it were my whim—

Her eyes fall on Simon. She starts—then indifferently.

Who is that lying at your feet? Your lover? Is he dead? Did you murder him for love of him? Oh, do not be afraid, I understand everything a woman's love could possibly compel her to desire. I know she can even kill herself to prove her love, so proud can she be of it.

SARA

Quietly.

I am sure you know that, My Lady.

> *She stares at Deborah and suddenly her face is convulsed with horrified suspicion and she grabs her by the arm and stammers.*

For the love of God, Deborah, tell me you're not just pretending now—for the love of him, to save him and set him free! That would be too great a price—

DEBORAH

> *With haughty anger—snatching Sara's hand off her arm.*

Do not presume to touch me! See that you take your lover away at once and never return here!

SARA

Yes, My Lady. But— Tell me this, are you happy now, My Lady?

DEBORAH

> *Smiles condescendingly.*

You are impertinent. But I forgive it, because I *am* happy.

> *She holds out her hand arrogantly.*

You may kneel and kiss my hand.

SARA

> *A flash of insulted pride comes to her eyes and for a second she seems about to retreat angrily—then impulsively she kneels and kisses her hand.*

Thank you for your great kindness, My Lady.

> *Deborah turns from her to ascend the steps. Sara adds huskily.*

And God bless you.

DEBORAH

> *Ascending the steps, looks back, with a smile of gracious understanding amusement.*

Why, thank you, good woman. I think that I may say that He has blessed me.

> *She goes into the summer-house and closes the door behind her.*

SARA

Stares after her—miserably.

I wonder—I wonder— Oh, God help me, I'll never be sure of the truth of it now!

Simon groans and stirs and looks up at her.

SIMON

Mother. Hurry! Let us go. Peace and happiness.

SARA

At once forgetting everything but him.

Yes, Darling. We'll go. Come on. Raise yourself.

She bends and puts her arm around his shoulder to help him.

That's it.

SIMON

Dazedly—like a little boy.

I fell and hit my head, Mother. It hurts.

SARA

I'll bathe it for you when we get in the house. Come along now.

She turns him into the path leading off left and urges him along it.

SIMON

Dazedly.

Yes, Mother.

SARA

With a fierce, passionate, possessive tenderness.

Yes, I'll be your Mother, too, now, and your peace and happiness and all you'll ever need in life! Come!

CURTAIN